Mobile Bühnen

Mobile Stages

Mobile Bühnen
Mobile Stages

Dirk Meyhöfer

avedition

Inhalt

Contents

Einleitung
Introduction

Architektonische Liebesgeschichten
Architectural love stories

Anmerkungen zu einem ungewöhnlichen Bautypus

Comments on an unusual type of construction

Mobile Bühnen bilden, wie Messestände oder Pavillons einer Weltausstellung, eine Unterart der Spezies »fliegende Bauten«[1]. Dieser kurze Satz ist gleichermaßen richtig wie auch verwirrend. | Denn fliegende Bauten sind – wie es sich in Deutschland gehört – in den entsprechenden Bauverordnungen als »bauliche Anlagen« festgelegt, die eben an verschiedenen Orten beliebig oft auf- und abgebaut werden dürfen. Eine eher unsentimentale, dafür praktische Definition. Doch irgendwie zutreffend. Niemand fliegt hier oder besitzt gar die dynamische Mobilität eines Flugzeuges oder Hochgeschwindigkeitszuges. | Und doch haben die »Fliegenden« unter den Bauten durch Epochen der Baugeschichte hindurch sich eine besondere, beinahe »erotische« Anziehungskraft auf ihre Schöpfer erarbeitet und schließlich behalten. Sie dürfen sich nämlich mit Attributen wie temporär, flüchtig und nicht seßhaft schmücken. Attribute, die sogenannte letzte Geheimnisse verbergen zu scheinen. Sie, die fliegenden Bauten, sind dynamisch – heute hier, morgen dort – und oft leben sie vom Mythos des »Gewesen sein«. Dabei stört nicht, daß sie provisorisch und oft improvisiert sind. Nein, je perfekter im Laufe des Industriezeitalters das Bauen möglich wurde, desto schneller entwickelte sich eine Sehnsucht zum Unvollkommenen. Es mag tatsächlich so sein – und dies ist meine These – daß diese fliegenden Bauten zur Love Affair für die meisten sie entwerfenden Architekten geworden sind. Das flüchtige Abenteuer, die Emotion, die hier die Rationalität überleben darf – das erinnert an Teenager-Lieben. Und jeder weiß, daß darunter oft die eine, die große war. | Ich weiß nicht, ob es einer wissenschaftlichen und ausführlichen Kulturgeschichte dieses Bautypus bedarf. Vielleicht mehr der pointierten Sammlung von Anmerkungen. (Eine eingängige Würdigung ist, soweit wirklich notwendig, bereits im Schwesterbuch »Fliegende Bauten – Der Messestand als konzeptionelle Aufgabe«[2] aufgeschrieben worden und sei zur Lektüre empfohlen.)

Es mag tatsächlich so sein, daß die fliegenden Bauten zur Love Affair für die meisten sie entwerfenden Architekten geworden sind.

Like trade-fair stands or the pavilions of a world exhibition, mobile stages are a sub-species of »temporary buildings«[1] . This short sentence is correct but confusing at the same time. | As is right and proper in Germany, temporary buildings are defined in the building regulations as constructions which can be erected and dismantled as frequently as desired and at different locations - an unsentimental and practical definition yet, nevertheless, to the point. The actual German designation is »fliegende Bauten«, meaning »flying buildings«, but the constructions referred to in the regulations do not fly, nor do they possess the dynamic mobility of an aeroplane or a high-speed train. | Nevertheless, throughout the epochs of architectural history, these »flying« constructions have gradually become endowed with and finally retained a special, almost »erotic« attraction for their creators. They are able to boast of their fleeting, volatile and rootless attributes, qualities which seem to conceal the final mysteries. These temporary, »flying« buildings are dynamic creatures, here today and gone tomorrow, and they often live on in a kind of mythology of the past. The fact that they are provisional and often simply improvised does not disturb this picture. On the contrary - the more perfected the activity of building became in the course of the industrial era, the faster a yearning grew for the incomplete, the imperfect. It may well be – and this is my thesis – that these temporary buildings have become partners in a love affair with the architects who are involved in designing them. The brief adventure, the emotions outlasting rationality, are reminiscent of teenage love. And, as everyone knows, this is often the love of our life. | I am not so sure whether a scientific and detailed cultural history of this type of building is required. More appropriate, perhaps, would be a selective collection of comments. (A trenchant homage, in so far as this is actually necessary, has already been paid in the form of a related book »Temporary Buildings – The Trade-Fair Stand as a Conceptional Challenge« [2], a volume which is well worth reading.)

Auch soll über den Begriff »Bühne« keine Flucht in die Tiefe des historischen Raumes erfolgen. Die Geschichte des Theater(baus) samt Bühne ist geschrieben. Und wie bei der dazu gehörigen »Software«, also dem Bühnenwerk der Antike, ist im Grunde auch die »Hardware« nachhaltig und für alle Zeiten in Griechenland und Rom definiert worden. Nichts ist mehr nach Orchestra (Bühne) und Skene (Bühnenhaus) neu zu erfinden gewesen; sollten wir die Widrigkeiten eines nordeuropäischen Klimas ausnehmen, die gewisse Schutzbauten gegen Kälte und Nässe erzwangen. Kein Stadion, kein Theaterbau, der sich nicht an den römischen Tribünenbautechniken des Auditoriums orientierte.[3] | Es gab im Laufe der Geschichte allerdings immer wieder Phasen, in denen das Theater von seinen eigentlichen gebauten Wirkungsstätten vertrieben wurde, so wie im frühen Mittelalter, als es den Theaterleuten verboten wurde, in den Kirchen zu spielen. Oder in der Moderne in den 60er Jahren unseres Jahrhunderts, als verkrustete gesellschaftliche Strukturen heilsam aufgebrochen wurden und konventionelle Spielorte verpönt waren. Es kam der unüberbrückbare Gegensatz zum Tragen zwischen der statischen Architektur und dem dynamischen Theater, das immer »Sichtbarmachen und eine ständige Revolution ist«, wie der britische Theatermann Peter Brook[4] schon 1968 reklamierte. Und: »An dem Tag, wo Theater statisch wird, beginnt etwas Unsichtbares zu sterben!« Das Spiel auf provisorischen Brettern, die ja die Welt bedeuten, kommt also dem Wesen des Theaters sehr nahe.

The concept of the »stage« should not trigger a flight into the depths of historical developments either. The history of theatre construction, which naturally includes the stage, has already been written. And as with the relevant »software«, namely the dramas of the ancient world, the »hardware« has also been defined for all time - in the Greece and Rome of antiquity. After orchestra (the semicircular space in front of the stage in ancient Greece) and scene (the area behind the proscenium, the stage itself or fly tower), there was nothing more to invent. If we leave out those parts of theatre construction intended to keep out the cold and rain produced by an adverse north-European climate, there is no single stadium or theatre building which is not oriented to the Roman construction techniques of the auditorium.[3] | In the course of history, however, there have always been phases when theatre has been driven out of the buildings created to house it, such as when theatre people were forbidden to put on their dramas in the churches of the Middle Ages. Or in modern times in the 60s of our century, when effete social structures were broken up in a process of healing and conventional locations for drama were seriously frowned upon. And then an unclosable gap appeared between static architecture and dynamic theatre, the latter always being »a process of visualisation and a continuous revolution«, as the British director Peter Brook[4] proclaimed as early as 1968. And »on the day when theatre becomes static, something invisible begins to die!« The phenomenon of drama on temporary wooden boards which are used to represent the world itself comes very close to the heart of what is theatre.

It may well be that these temporary buildings have become partners in a love affair with the architects who are involved in designing them.

Im Kern ist das Entstehen und der Bestand der mobilen Bühnen so beschrieben: Im Mittelalter, als sowohl kirchliche Akteure wie auch die profanen Straßenkünstler in unterschiedlichen Genres die Weltprobleme als historische Legenden, Schäferspiele, Mysterien oder Possen simultan verdichteten, wurde ein beweglicher Bauernkarren provisorisch ausstaffiert, manchmal auch schlecht und grell geschmückt. | Mobile Bühnen, wenn ich das so zusammenfassen darf, erlebten einen Quantensprung in dem Augenblick, als das industrielle Zeitalter neue Baumaterialien (Eisen, später Stahl, Aluminium, Kunststoffe) und -konstruktionen hervorbrachte, die den »Leiterwagen« ablösen konnten. Als erstes profitierte das Zelt, die Mutter aller fliegenden Bauten in der Abteilung bildende Kunst, davon. Die Stangen eines Tipi, Birkenkegels oder Kata mußten nicht mehr aus schwerem Holz, sondern durften aus schlankem Stahl sein. Diese konnten dann wiederum Zeltkonstruktionen in einer Größenordnung tragen, die viel mehr als einer Handvoll Leute Platz boten. | Die Architekten des 20. Jahrhunderts, und vor allem die Utopisten unter ihnen, beschränkten sich nicht auf das Thema Zelt. Was die Baumeister von den Theaterleuten lernen konnten, war die Tatsache, daß ein Theaterstück immer die Verdichtung, Überhöhung und Quintessenz eines real existierenden Menschheitsproblems ist. Manchmal, wenn das Theaterstück genial ist, eben die Abstraktion auf das Wesentliche. »Weniger ist mehr«, meldet sich ganz tief hinten im Gehirn die entsprechende Äußerung des Protagonisten der Moderne, Mies van der Rohe.

Was die Baumeister von den Theaterleuten lernen konnten, war die Tatsache, daß ein Theaterstück immer die Verdichtung, Überhöhung und Quintessenz eines real existierenden Menschheitsproblems ist.

In essence, the origins and continuity of mobile stages can be described in exactly the same way. In the Middle Ages, when both ecclesiastical actors and their secular counterparts, the street performers, simultaneously condensed the problems of the life as historical legends, pastoral plays, mysteries or farces, a movable farmers cart would be dressed up, sometimes badly and garishly decorated. | Mobile stages, if I may summarise them as such, experienced a quantum leap at the moment when the industrial era brought forth new building materials (iron, later steel, aluminium, plastics) and constructions which were able to take over from the »horse-driven cart«. The first to profit from this was the tent, the mother of all temporary buildings in the area of fine arts. The rods of a teepee, a cone or catafalque no longer had to be made of heavy wood but, instead, of slender steel. Tent constructions were thus enabled of a size to accommodate more than just a handful of people. | The architects of the 20th century, and especially the utopians among them, did not limit themselves to the tent. What they were able to learn from theatre people was the fact that a play is always a condensation, exaggeration and quintessence of a human problem which exists in reality. Sometimes, when the play is a work of genius, it is an abstraction of an

What they were able to learn from theatre people was the fact that a play is always a condensation, exaggeration and quintessence of a human problem which exists in reality.

Modellhafte Abstraktion also hieß das Thema für Architekten und später für Designer. Das paßt und ist willkommen. Es gibt in der klassischen Architektenausbildung die Aufgabe des Stegreifentwurfes, eine konzentrierte Fingerübung innerhalb einer vorgegebenen Zeit. Auch der Architektenwettbewerb fordert vom Teilnehmer nicht die Durcharbeitung bis zum Detail im Maßstab 1:1. Nein, vor allem die grundlegende Idee, die Vision, ist das Ziel. Architekten wollen zwar bauen, konstruieren und detaillieren, aber manchmal reichen ihnen auch Gedankengebäude. Die Aufgabe, eine temporäre Bühne zu gestalten, kommt dem entgegen, läßt Platz für das kreative Element des Baukünstlers. | Lange bevor moderne Materialien es zuließen, mobile Großbühnen beispielsweise für die Rolling Stones zu bauen, hatten sich die Architekten schon auf das Bühnenbild kapriziert, also den ohnehin immer mobilen Teil der Bühne. Viele berühmte Baumeister haben sich damit beschäftigt. Allen voran sicher der preußische Staatsbaumeister Karl Friedrich Schinkel (1781-1841). Dessen umfassende Begabungen versetzten diese klassizistische Lichtgestalt in die wohl einmalige glückliche Konstellation, nicht nur das neue Berliner Schauspielhaus (nach dem Brand des alten um 1817, errichtet in den Jahren 1818 - 1821) zu erbauen, sondern dort und anderswo etwa auch 100 Bühnendekorationen für mehr als 30 Stücke zu arrangieren.

essence. »Less is more« was the message of that protagonist of the modern, Mies van der Rohe, a message which has sunk in deep. | Modelled abstraction was therefore the theme for architects and later for designers – a fitting and welcome innovation. A classic component of architectural studies is the improvised design, a concentrated learning technique to be performed within a stipulated time. Even architectural competitions do not require of the participants that they draw up plans in detail on a scale of 1 to 1. The underlying idea, the vision itself is the goal. Architects may want to build, to construct and to go into the details, but sometimes they are satisfied with a mental conception of a building. The task of designing a temporary stage comes close to such a process and leaves room for the creative component of the architect's being. | Long before modern materials allowed the construction of large mobile stages, for the Rolling Stones for example, architects had already taken over the design of stage sets, the part of the stage which is always mobile. Many famous master builders have involved themselves in this field, the first being, without doubt, the Prussian master builder, Karl Friedrich Schinkel (1781 - 1841). His comprehensive talents put this shining light of classicism in the unique and fortunate position of not only being commissioned to build the new Berlin playhouse (built in the years 1818 to 1821 after the old one burnt down in 1817) but also to design the scenery for around 100 other stages with more than 30 plays.

Schinkel versammelte Begabungen und Fähigkeiten des praktizierenden Baumenschen und kombinierte sie mit jenen des raffinierten und gebildeten Malers und Zeichners. »Er hatte alle Baustile studiert und vermochte sie seiner nie versiegenden Phantasie dienstbar zu machen. Sein bühnenreformerischer Erfolg lag in der Ablösung von barocken Kulissenbauten durch eine illusionistische Hintergrundmalerei, den Prospekt«, schrieb Ursula Rieman-Reher 1982[5]. Das wohl bekannteste seiner Bühnenbilder, das inzwischen weltweit als Plakat publiziert wurde, ist sein Entwurf zur Inszenierung des 2. Bildes im 1. Akt der Zauberflöte von Wolfgang Amadeus Mozart. Dort erscheint die Königin auf einer Mondsichel unter einem tiefblauen Firmament. Es ist das illusionistische Bild einer riesigen Kuppel, einer der Archeformen der Architektur seit dem römischen Pantheon, oder wie der Autor Carletoon Coon schrieb: »Man ist fast versucht zu sagen, daß die kuppelartig gewölbte Hütte für den Menschen kulturspezifisch so bezeichnend ist, wie das Drosselnest für die Drossel«[6]. Schinkels Kuppel im Alten Museum ist immer noch eines der schönsten gebauten Exemplare. | Andere Bühnenentwürfe Schinkels bilden andere starke Architekturmotive ab. Und dabei tun sich überraschende Parallelen zu seinem übrigen Werk auf: Seine Visionen für einen Palast am Meer in Orianda könnten Bühnenkulissen sein, wie der Entwurf zum Sonnen-

Schinkel hat mit seinen Bühnenbildern zweidimensionale Raumbilder geschaffen. Nicht Räume zum Leben, sondern Räume zum Erahnen und zur Illusion.

Schinkel was a collector of the gifts and skills of practising builders, and combined them with those of sophisticated and learned painters and drawers. »He had studied all architectural styles and was able to adapt them to the service of his unbounded imagination. His success in changing the face of the stage was to be found in his replacement of baroque scenery constructions with illusionist background painting, the back-drop«, wrote Ursula Rieman-Reher in 1982[5]. His probably most well-known stage set, now available as a poster all over the world, is his design for staging the 2nd scene in Act 1 of the Magic Flute by Wolfgang Amadeus Mozart. Here, the queen appears on a crescent moon beneath a deep-blue firmament. It is the illusionistic picture of a huge dome, one of the arch shapes of architecture since the Roman Pantheon, or, as author Carletoon Coon once wrote: »It is almost tempting to say that the dome-type vaulted abode is as typical for the culture of humankind as the thrush's nest is for the thrush«[6] . Schinkel's dome in the Alte Museum is still one of the most beautiful examples of its kind ever built. | Other stage designs of Schinkel reflect other strong architectural motifs. And surprising parallels to the rest of his work are also apparent: his visions for a palace on the coast in Orianda could well be stage backgrounds, such as his design of the sun temple for The Magic Flute, with the temple as utopia. Schinkel created two-dimensional »spatial images« with his stage sets. Not

tempel für die Zauberflöte eine Utopie sein könnte. Schinkel hat mit seinen Bühnenbildern zweidimensionale »Raumbilder« geschaffen. Nicht Räume zum Leben, sondern Räume zum Erahnen und zur Illusion. Das Sujet der »Bühne« fordert dazu heraus, und heute am Ende des 20. Jahrhunderts können wir noch ganz andere Annäherungen seitens der (Bau-)Künstler verzeichnen. | Die Beschäftigung mit dem Raum ist so alt wie die gesamte abendländische Baugeschichte. Sie beginnt nicht etwa erst mit den Raumwundern der gotischen Kathedralen. Aber mit ihnen wird doch schon eine vierte Dimension des Raumes, jene der Überhöhung und des Symbolisierens deutlich. Jede Epoche wird dann gemäß ihrer eigenen Vorstellungen mit dem Raum in Architektur und Stadt umgehen. Spätestens in der Moderne, also im 20. Jahrhundert, beginnt der Raum-Begriff zu »fliegen«, ein »unendlicher, losgelöster, ätherischer Raum entsteht«, wie Frank Werner[7] schreibt, »als die Wolkenbügelhäuser von El Lissitzky erdacht werden.« | Über den Raum als zentrale Idee, Aufgabe und letztendlich auch als Trauma der Architekten und aller anderen, die eine sinnliche Beziehung zur Architektur aufgebaut haben, intensiver nachzudenken, sprengt den Rahmen dieser Publikation. Es bleibt jedoch die wichtige Erkenntnis, daß es immer wieder der Raum ist, den es gilt, auf der Bühne und über der Bühne zu zelebrieren. Denn temporär einen »Raum« aufzubauen und zu formulieren, läßt dem Architekten mehr Spielraum als bei einem Bauwerk aus Stein, Mörtel, Holz oder Beton.

spaces to live in but spaces of presentiment and illusion. The subject of the »stage« is the challenge to achieve just this and today, at the end of the 20th century, we can see completely different approaches being adopted by the (architectural) artist. | Fascination with the idea of spatial design is as old as the whole history of Occidental architecture. It did not begin with the miracles of Gothic cathedrals but they can clearly be associated with a fourth dimension of space, that of exalted heights and symbolism. Each epoch thus deals with concept of space in architecture and the city according to its own particular ideas. At the latest in the modern period, namely in the 20th century, the concept of enclosed space began to »take wing«, an »unending, unbound ethereal space develops«, as Frank Werner[7] wrote in a homage to the architect and artist, Dieter Schaal, »as when the cloud-shaped houses of El Lissitzky are imagined.« | To think more intensively about space as the central idea, task and finally trauma of architects and all others who have developed a sensuous relationship to architecture goes beyond the scope of this book. The important realisation remains, however, that it is always space which to be celebrated, on and over the stage. For to construct and formulate a »space« temporarily leaves the architect more room for creativity than is the case with buildings made of stone, mortar, wood or concrete.

Schinkel created two-dimensional »spatial images« with his stage sets. Not spaces to live in but spaces of presentiment and illusion.

Architekten wie Hans Dieter Schaal nun sind wahre Raumkünstler und begreifen zum Beispiel den Raum nicht nur als »kubikmetrische« Einheit. Schaals Wegräume, Kopfräume, vegetabilen und versteinerten Räume, Geburts-, Toten- und Körperräume – um nur einige zu nennen – »all das sind Gebilde, die erst durch Interaktionen zum Zeichen, zum Symbolraum, zum dechiffrierbaren archaischen Fundgut werden.«[8] Dieser Schaal wird im 5. Akt dieses Buches seine Raumtheorien auf der Bühne präsentieren. Man kann dies als eine der möglichen Fortführungen Schinkels begreifen, als mobile Installationen zum Thema »Bühnenarchitektur«, oder »Architektur für das Theater«. | Das Thema der mobilen Bühnen als »fliegender Bau« reicht viel tiefer an die Fundamente der Architekturtheorie und -philosophie heran, als vordergründig vermutet werden darf. Besonders zeitgenössische Architekten haben sich sehr gern auf dieses Thema eingelassen. Es sei noch einmal daran erinnert, daß der Kern einer Idee hier ungefilterter zum Ausdruck kommt. Klar, daß Architektur nicht nur zur Bühne für Spiel, Schau- oder Singspiel wird. Nein: sie wird auch zur Bühne eigener Visionen. Das reicht von opulenten show-cases eines Matteo Thun oder Mario Botta bis zum kafkaesken Mikrokosmos mit scharfkantigen, spitzen Metallgebirgen, einem Irrgarten, wie ihn Daniel Libeskind zur Präsentation seiner eigenen Projekte auf einer Rotterdamer Ausstellung benutzt. Die »mobile Bühne« konnte sich in ihrer Übersetzung ins Reale den allgemeinen Tendenzen in der Baukunst natürlich nicht entziehen – im Gegenteil: Sie wird zur Präsentation mit Ausrufungszeichen – zum Denkmal der

Klar, daß Architektur nicht nur zur Bühne für Spiel, Schau- oder Singspiel wird. Nein: sie wird auch zur Bühne eigener Visionen.

Hans Dieter Schaal is a veritable artist of space and comprehends space not merely as a »cubic« unit. His way rooms, head rooms, vegetable and petrified rooms, his birth, death and body rooms – to name but a few – are »all structures which only through interaction turn into signs, symbolic space, decodable archaic treasures.«[8] In Act 5 of this book, this Schaal will present his theories of space on the stage of the written word. This can be understood as one of the possible continuations of Schinkel, as a series of mobile installations on the topic of »stage architecture« or »architecture for the theatre«. | The topic of mobile stages as »temporary buildings« reaches much further down into the foundations of architectural theory and philosophy than can be suspected on first consideration. Contemporary architects especially have taken pleasure in involving themselves in this topic. It should be remembered once again that this is the best way to express the nucleus of an idea. It is, of course, clear that architecture does not only become a stage for acting, drama or opera. On the contrary, it also becomes the stage of the architect's own visions. This ranges from the opulent show-cases of a Matteo Thun or Mario Botta to the kafkaesque microcosms with sharp-edged, pointed metal mountains, a maze such as the one used by Daniel Libes-

It is, of course, clear that architecture does not only become a stage for acting, drama or opera. On the contrary, it also becomes the stage of the architect's own visions.

Strömungen und Störungen, der Ein- und Aussichten. Die Architektur des 20. Jahrhunderts, dort besonders dessen zweiter Hälfte, dreht sich sehr schnell, und am Ende stand die Erkenntnis, daß alles möglich ist! So natürlich auch als und auf der Bühne. | Das Denken über Architektur und Raum erreicht dabei konsequenterweise Grenzen, wie eine aktuelle Äußerung des Schweizer Architekten Niklaus Fritschi beweist: »Es ist der Traum des entmaterialisierten, offen fließenden Raumes, der die Architektur des ausgehenden Jahrtausends prägt – die gläserne Membrane als Element der Klimakontrolle in Analogie zur menschlichen Haut, die fast materiallos das Innen vom Außen abgrenzt und gleichzeitig Kontaktorgan ist.«[9] | Das Zitat ist eine Brücke hin zu einer sich just wandelnden Architekturszene, die an einer prägnanten Schwelle angekommen ist. Städte scheinen ihre Zukunft nur noch im virtuellen Internet zu suchen, Bildschirm-Architekturen lösen womöglich bald steinerne Bauwerke ab. Die Einheit von Raum und Zeit, das Hier und Jetzt, das jahrhundertelang integraler Bestandteil jeder Architekturkonzeption war, ist bedroht.

kind to present his own projects at a Rotterdam exhibition. The »mobile stage«, when translated into reality, is unable to escape general trends in the art of architecture. On the contrary, it becomes a method of presentation with exclamation marks, a monument to the spirit of the times – to upheavals, to insight and to outlook. The architecture of the 20th century, especially the second half, has been transforming itself at breakneck speed and, in the end, there is the realisation that everything is possible – as and on the stage. | It is here that thought about architecture and space reach certain limits, as a recent remark of the Swiss architect, Niklaus Fritschi, demonstrates: »It is the dream of de-materialised, openly flowing spaces which typifies the architecture of a millennium that is coming to a close – the glass membrane as an element of climate control, as an analogy to the human skin, which almost insubstantially delimits the outside from the inside and, at the same time, is an organ of contact.«[9] | This quotation can be taken as a bridge to a wandering architectural scene that has arrived at a pregnant threshold. Cities now seem to be looking for their future only within the virtual internet, whereby screen architecture may well soon replace constructions made of stone. The unity of space and time, the here and now, which has been an integral component of all architectural thinking for hundreds of years, is now being threatened.

Wir wissen nicht, wohin das führen kann. Aber wir besitzen möglicherweise Hinweise und Beispiele. Sie sind zu finden in der ohnehin global angelegten Pop-Kultur. Bühnen(bilder) für die Rolling Stones werden vorab weltweit im Internet und via Popsender wie MTV transportiert. Sie sind virtuell, bevor sie für einen einzigen Abend in Los Angeles, Krakau, Manila oder Rio de Janeiro gebaute Wirklichkeit werden. Die Disziplin »Stage Architecture« ist eine Kreuzung aus fliegendem Bau und Multimedia. Für mich ist sie eine Art Königsdisziplin: zeitgeistig und zielorientiert. Sie fußt auf einer High-Tech-Konstruktion, die in Stunden montiert und wieder demontiert werden kann. | Ja – es ist ein Arbeiten am Limit: Innenarchitektur wird zur Architektur, Kulisse zum Gebauten, Reales zu Virtuellem und dann zu Multimedia. | Noch werden die Bühnenträume von den Stones, Tina Turner oder Michael Jackson wirklich gebaut. Vielleicht kann man sich das bald schon sparen: Denn die Computeranimationen vorab kommen der späteren Realität inzwischen sehr nahe. Willkommen beim Cyber Rock-Konzert anywhere – willkommen zur virtuellen Bühne, die durch die endlose Cybernet World fliegt … .

Die Disziplin Stage Architecture ist eine Kreuzung aus fliegendem Bau und Multimedia. Sie ist eine Art Königsdisziplin: zeitgeistig und zielorientiert.

We do not know where this will lead us. But there are some indications and examples. They are to be found in the globally entrenched pop culture. Stage sets for the Rolling Stones will from now on be transported world-wide on the internet and via music stations such as MTV. They only exist as virtual entities before actually being built for a single evening in Los Angeles, Krakow, Manila or Rio de Janeiro. As a discipline, Stage Architecture is a hybrid of temporary building and multimedia. For me, it is a kind of royal discipline: with the spirit of the times and oriented to specific goals. It is based on high-tech construction which can be assembled and dismantled again within hours. | This is what is meant by working at the limit. Interior architecture becomes architecture, the backdrop becomes the building, the real becomes the virtual and then all becomes multimedia. | The stage dreams of the Stones, Tina Turner or Michael Jackson are still being built in reality but perhaps this will soon be unnecessary as computer animation is already coming very close to what will later be accepted as reality. Welcome to the anywhere cyber rock concert – welcome to the virtual stage which flies through the endless Cybernet World … .

As a discipline, Stage Architecture is a hybrid of temporary building and multimedia. It is a kind of royal discipline: with the spirit of the times and oriented to specific goals.

[1] … vgl. auch Karin Schulte: Fliegende Bauten, Stuttgart 1997. Dieses Buch verarbeitet einen wesentlichen Teil der Abteilung Fliegende Bauten; hier mehr die kommerziellen Messebauten.

[2] … ebd. In diesem Buch ist ein historischer Abriß erschienen, der auch für dieses Kapitel weitgehend Bedeutung hat. Um Doubletten zu vermeiden, verzichten wir auf einen weiteren historischen Abriß.

[3] … vgl. auch Lexikon der Weltarchitektur, München 1992.

[4] … vgl. Gaelle Breton: Theater, Stuttgart u. Zürich 1990, S. 4ff.

[5] … Karl Friedrich Schinkel – eine Ausstellung der DDR, Berlin 1992, S. 181ff.

[6] … Torwald Faegre: Zelte, Hamburg 1980.

[7] … Architektonische Situationen, Zeichnungen und Überlegungen von H.D. Schaal, Stuttgart 1980.

[8] … ebd.

[9] … Dirk Meyhöfer, Architectural Visions for Europe, Wiesbaden 1994, im Aufsatz: Genesis und Karriere … .

[1] … cf. Karin Schulte: Temporary Buildings, Stuttgart 1997. This book deals with another aspect of temporary buildings with the emphasis on commercial trade-fair stands.

[2] … ibid. In this book, there is a historical outline which is also extensively significant for this chapter. In order to avoid duplications, we will dispense with a historical synopsis.

[3] … cf. Lexikon der Weltarchitektur, Munic 1992.

[4] … cf. Gaelle Breton: Theater, Stuttgart and Zürich 1990, S. 4ff.

[5] … Karl Friedich Schinkel – eine Ausstellung der DDR, Berlin 1992, S. 181ff.

[6] … Torwald Faegre: Zelte, Hamburg 1980.

[7] … Architektonische Situationen Zeichnungen und Überlegungen von H. D. Schaal, Stuttgart 1980.

[8] … ibid.

[9] … Dirk Meyhöfer Architectural Visions for Europe, Wiesbaden 1994, in the essay: Genesis und Karriere … .

1. Akt
Act 1

Unter der Zelthaut – verzaubert

Under the skin and spellbound

Der größte in Europa: Circus Krone

Roncalli: das achte Zeltwunder

Bar jeder Vernunft: zur Zeit Berlin

Millenniumsstart im Zelt: London 2000

The Krone circus: the largest of its kind in Europe

Roncalli: the eighth tent wonder of the world

Bar jeder Vernunft: Berlin now

Starting the millennium in a tent: London 2000

Der 1. Akt im klassischen Schauspiel ist die Exposition. Sie dient der »Darstellung und Entwicklung der für den Konflikt oder die Katastrophe in der Tragödie notwendigen Voraussetzungen« (»Grundbegriffe der Literatur«, Frankfurt/M. 1966). Übertragen auf das Thema der mobilen Bühnen, ist es die Ein- und Hinführung. In diesem 1. Akt spielt der Archetypus Zelt die Hauptrolle. Das Zelt gilt als bewegliche Heimstatt der Nomaden, das Zelt wurde aber auch zum Bühnenschutz des fahrenden Volks. | Es war eine sinnvolle Ehe, die dort geschlossen wurde, denn ein Großteil der Ur-Zeltkonstruktionen ist rund oder ellipsoid, sozusagen sui generis als Dach für Bühne und Auditorium für den Typus »Circus« geeignet, wie ihn die Antike kannte. In der Zeit der Frühindustrialisierung und der Hand in Hand gehenden Entwicklung, nun mehr Rohstoffe wie Holz im großen Stil mechanisch bearbeiten zu können, entstanden aus der kleinteiligen Jahrmarkt- und Schaustellerszene früherer Jahrhunderte jetzt größere Unternehmungen. Der Typus Wanderzirkus war geboren. Die Menschen wohnten nun mehr und mehr dicht gedrängt in Städten und Siedlungen. Ein stetig wachsendes Potential an Menschen suchte eine Unterbrechung ihres tristen Arbeitslebens. Schon bald nach dem Ersten Weltkrieg existierten »wandernde« Zeltkonstruktionen, die 6.000 Menschen Platz boten. | Die Aufgabe ist klar: Zum Brot die Spiele – »Menschen, Tiere, Sensationen« im Zirkus versprachen im Frühkapitalismus das, was heute omnipotente Freizeit- und Abenteuerparks leisten.

Die Welt des Zirkus ist eine Welt des Glanzes und der Illusionen, aber sie ist auch von harter Arbeit und vom alltäglichen Lebenskampf geprägt.

The 1st act in classical Greek drama is the exposition. Its purpose is to »present and develop the necessary preconditions for the conflict or the catastrophe in the tragedy« (»Grundbegriffe der Literatur«, Frankfurt/M. 1966). Transferred to the topic of mobile stages, this is both introduction and lead-on. In this 1st act, the archetype of the tent, the outer skin, plays the main role in our drama. The tent is the movable home of the nomads but it also became a way of protecting the stages of strolling players. | It was a beneficial marriage which was consummated at the time, since a majority of the ancient tent constructions were round or ellipsoid, so to say suitable sui generis as both a roof over the stage and as an auditorium for the circus, a designation already in use in the ancient world. In the time of early industrialisation and the parallel development of machinery for working a larger variety of materials such as wood in large quantities, the small-scale fairground and circus scene of earlier centuries was now able to expand its dimensions – the travelling circus was born. Now, people were living squashed more and more closely together in cities and settlements. A continually growing population sought an escape from the misery of their dreary working lives. Not long after the First World War, there were travelling circus constructions with room for 6,000 people.

Der Zirkus war (und ist wieder) eine Einrichtung, die zum Menschen kommen konnte, also beweglich sein mußte. Der Archetypus Zelt bildet dafür eine ideale Illusionskulisse: »Die Welt des Zirkus« schreibt Olaf Bartels, der Biograph des Circus Krone, »ist eine Welt des Glanzes und der Illusionen, aber sie ist auch von harter Arbeit und vom alltäglichen Lebenskampf geprägt. In jedem Zirkuszelt spiegelt sich dieses Verhältnis. Jeden Abend erstrahlen ihre nüchternen Gestänge und Stoffe im bunten Lichterglanz, und es lockt die reich verzierte Fassade vor dem kargen Zelt mit ihren Lampen zum Eintritt.« | Ja, es sind einfache Mittel, die benutzt werden, brennende Kerzen, dazu die Farbe Rot; dann Spiegel, immer wieder Spiegel, die die halbdunkle Welt mystifizieren. Und die Kraft der Kuppel und des Kreises leistet ihr Übriges. Was ist logischer, als in einem Zelt den Beginn des neuen Jahrtausends zu feiern?

Their purpose was clear: to sweeten the bitter pill. In early capitalism, »people, animals, sensations» in the circus promised that which, today, the omnipotent leisure and adventure parks offer. The circus was (and is again) an institution that could come to the people and therefore had to be mobile. The tent as an archetype was the ideal background for the illusion presented. »The world of the circus», wrote Olaf Bartels, the biographer of the Circus Krone, »is a world of glamour and illusion, but it is also characterised by hard work and the everyday struggle to survive. This relationship is reflected in every circus tent. Each evening, the normally down-to-earth poles and circus materials shine in the colourful glitter of lights; the lights of the richly decorated facade interrupting the otherwise dull exterior lures passers-by inside. | The means applied are simple: some burning candles, the colour red and mirror upon mirror used to mystify a world of semi-darkness. And the power of the dome and the circle does the rest. What is more logical than to celebrate the beginning of the new millennium in a tent?

The world of the circus is a world of glamour and illusion, but it is also characterised by hard work and the everyday struggle to survive.

Die mobile Zirkuswelt zu Beginn des 20. Jahrhunderts: mit Kuppel und dreiteiligem Fassadenaufbau eine perfekte Adaption historischer Vorbilder aus der Geschichte fester Bauten.

The mobile circus world at the beginning of the 20 C - with its cupolas and three-section facade, a perfect adaptation of its historical precursor, the stationary building.

Der größte in Europa: Circus Krone

The Krone circus: the largest of its kind in Europe

Der Circus Krone unterhält als einziger deutscher Großzirkus in München einen festen Sitz, den Circus-Krone-Bau (Architekt: Ludwig Galitz, 1962), in dem in jedem Jahr vom 25. Dezember bis zum März des folgenden Jahres internationale Programme gezeigt werden. Das Zirkuszelt des Unternehmens, wo der Begriff Wanderzirkus verpönt ist und man statt dessen Zeltzirkus sagt, kann 5.000 Personen aufnehmen. Zusammen mit der Gesamtexpedition aus 250 Tieren, 400 Menschen, 330 Wohn- und Gepäckwagen wird jeweils eine Fläche von drei Hektar belegt, wenn der Zirkus einen neuen Ort besucht. Die mobile Bühne zieht als Tross eine gesamte mobile Stadt hinter sich her.

Krone is the only large circus company in Germany to maintain offices at a fixed location in Munich, the Circus Krone building (architect: Ludwig Galitz, 1962). Each year, from 25 December to March of the following year, an international program is presented. The company's circus tent – where the term »travelling circus« is frowned upon and »tent circus« is preferred – can accommodate 5,000 people. Whenever the circus visits a city, it requires an area of three hectares for the 250 animals, 400 people and 330 caravans and luggage transporters. The mobile stage, in the form of a baggage train, tows along a whole mobile city in its wake.

Rechts: Die Manege hat einen Durchmesser von 12,50 Meter und wird von einem roten Ring begrenzt, der beleuchtet ist und das Netz für den Raubtierkäfig enthält. Über der Manege agieren die Luftartisten.
Unten: Auftritt auf drei Ebenen: in der Manege, auf der Bühne und in der Luft. Die Bühne ist faltbar und besitzt 1,20 Meter hohe Bühnentreppen.

Right: The diameter of the arena is 12.5 metres. It is encircled by a red illuminated ring and contains the net for the animal cage. Above the arena is where the high-wire acrobats perform.
Below: There are three different levels: the arena, the stage and in the air. The stage can be divided and has a 1.20 metre-high staircase.

Roncalli: das achte Zeltwunder

Roncalli: the eighth tent wonder of the world

Nüchternes Gestänge, dank heutigen Wissens und Forschung schlank und rank auf ein Minimum reduziert, so daß niemandem der 600 Zuschauer mehr die Sicht genommen werden muß. Das »achte Zeltwunder«, wie die Roncallis ihr High Tech-Zelt gern nennen, wird durch opulentes Dekor konterkariert: Roncalli hat sich – ob für Programmheft oder Logengestühl – der Farbe Rot ergeben. Seit dem Beginn 1976 setzt Roncalli auf die Wiedergeburt des poetischen Zirkus, und entsprechend muß eben die Kulisse sein. Deswegen wurde 1994 ein historischer Artistenzugang eingefügt. Dessen gedrechselte Holzsäulen und der rot kaschierte Samt ist während der Vorstellungen der überwältigende Orientierungspunkt für die Zuschauer, der »Schlund«, der unaufhörlich Menschen, Tiere und Sensationen ausspuckt.

Thanks to research and present-day skills, the supporting rods are plain and thin, reduced to a minimum so that none of the 600 spectators are prevented from enjoying the show. The eighth tent wonder, as the Roncallis like to call their high-tech tent, is counterpointed by opulent decoration, with everything in red – from the program leaflet to the seats in the boxes. Since the beginning of 1976, Roncalli has presented itself as the rebirth of the poetic circus and the decor was selected to support this image. It was for this very reason that, in 1994, a historical artistes' entrance was added. Its elaborate wooden columns and the red velvet cladding is a point of orientation for the audience during the performances, a »maw« that continuously spits out people, animals and sensations.

Rechts: Historischer Artistenzugang mit gedrechselten Holzsäulen und rot kaschiertem Samt.
Nächste Seiten: Totale – freie Sicht für alle Zuschauer.

Right: Historical artistes' entrance with ornamental wooden columns and red velvet.
Following pages: Clear view for all the audience.

Bar jeder Vernunft: zur Zeit Berlin

Bar jeder Vernunft: Berlin now

Man braucht schon einen Kompaß, um einen der neuen Kultorte des Berliner Nachtlebens in der Nähe des Kurfürstendamms zu finden, der versteckt auf dem Parkdeck der ehemaligen Freien Volksbühne in Wilmersdorf liegt. Von außen betrachtet, ist er eher mit dem Charme einer wandernden Schrebergartensiedlung behaftet, innen ist der Aha-Effekt umso größer: Die Stars der deutschen und internationalen Kleinkunst, von Chanson über Kabarett und Jazz bis zur Comedy, haben sich ein Kleinod europäischer Zeltbaukunst ausgesucht, um ihre Künste intim und direkt zur Aufführung zu bringen. Es handelt sich daher um ein Spiegelzelt, von denen es zur Zeit auf der Welt nur noch etwa acht Exemplare gibt. Es stammt aus Belgien und heißt programmatisch »Danse Palais«. Die Holzrotunde wurde in Handarbeit zu Beginn des Jahrhunderts gefertigt. Jugendstilornamentik ist sichtbar. Die Holztäfelungen zusammen mit den geschliffenen Spiegelgläsern sowie die mit Samt ausgeschlagenen Logen verführen zu einer gewagten, aber richtigen Feststellung: Dies ist ein guter Platz für die Nacht, für das Vergnügen. Die Künstler, die hier auftreten, bestätigen dies genauso wie die begeisterten Zuschauer.

In the vicinity of the Kurfürstendamm, you really need a compass to find one of Berlin's new cult locations which is to be found hidden on the parking level of the former Freie Volksbühne in Wilmersdorf. Viewed from the outside, it has more of the charm of a travelling collection of garden plots but, inside, the surprise is all the greater. The stars of German and international cabaret, jazz and comedy sought out a gem of European tent architecture to present themselves and their performances. It is a mirror tent, of which there are only around eight examples in the whole world. It originates from Belgium and is appropriately called the »Danse Palais«. The wooden rotunda was made by hand at the beginning of the century and the art nouveau ornamentation is still plain to see. The wooden panels, together with the polished mirrors and the boxes cladded with velvet, seduce the visitor into making a daring but truthful discovery: that this is an agreeable place for the night and for pleasure. The artistes who appear here confirm this, as does the enthusiastic audience as well.

Geschickt vergrößern die umlaufenden Spiegel den realen Raum – zumindest virtuell.

The surrounding mirrors skilfully magnify the actual space – at least virtually.

Links: Außen ein informativer, reißerischer Auftakt – wie er schon auf den historischen Jahrmärkten üblich war.
Rechts: Innen erinnert die textile, flexible Struktur des Zeltdachs an die vergängliche Beweglichkeit einer »fliegenden« Bauweise.

Left: Outside, an informative but alluring entrance – as was usual at the fairs of the past.
Right: Inside, the textile and flexible structure of the tent's roof is a reminder of the transitory nature of temporary buildings.

Millenniumsstart im Zelt: London 2000

Starting the millennium in a tent: London 2000

Richard Rogers und Mark Fisher

Mit einer Investition von einer dreiviertel Milliarde Pfund ist der Millennium Dome (Entwurf Richard Rogers) das größte Einzelprojekt innerhalb der britischen Unternehmungen zum Jahrtausendwechsel. Bei der zeltartigen Konstruktion mit einer Höhe von etwa 50 und einem Durchmesser von 320 Metern dürfte es sich um das wohl größte Zelt der Welt handeln. Immerhin würde Londons traditionelles Wembley Stadion zweimal dort hineinpassen. Im engeren Sinne ist das Festzelt kein »fliegender Bau«, weil es sehr wahrscheinlich die kalkulierte Lebensdauer von etwa 25 Jahren in Greenwich, östlich der City of London, auf der imaginären Achse des Null-Meridians stehen wird. Prinzipiell ist der Millennium Dome jedoch durchaus als Mitglied der Familie Zelt zu bezeichnen. Im neuen Jahrtausend wird im äußeren Ring ein üppiger Themenpark mit 14 Ausstellungszonen präsentiert. Der Nukleus ist einem Auditorium für eine Multimedia-Show vorbehalten. Mark Fisher, der Bühnenarchitekt der Rolling Stones, soll diese Show inszenieren. Wie alles genau aussehen wird, ob vielleicht, nach einem Vorschlag von David Hockney, doch der Innenraum völlig leer bleibt – am 1. Januar 2000 fallen spätestens die Vorhänge und enthüllen die Millennium Show.

With an investment of three-quarters of a billion pounds, the Millennium Dome (design by Richard Rogers) is the largest single project of British enterprise towards the end of the last thousand years. It is the largest tent in the world, being 50 metres high and 320 metres in diameter; even London's traditional Wembley Stadium would fit into it twice. It is not really a temporary building, in the narrow sense of the word, because it will probably remain on the imaginary axis of the prime meridian in Greenwich in the east of London for the whole of its calculated lifetime of 25 years. In principle, however, the Millennium Dome can certainly be described as a member of the tent family. In the new millennium a spacious theme park with 14 exhibition zones will be presented in the outer ring. The nucleus is reserved for an auditorium for a multi-media show. Mark Fisher, the stage designer for the Rolling Stones, is to stage-manage this show. How everything will look exactly and whether the interior will remain entirely empty, as David Hockney has proposed, will be revealed on 1 January 2000 when the curtains rise on the show of the millennium.

Das Millennium-Zelt in der Aufbauphase. Bananenförmige Stahlstützen tragen die an Seilen aufgehängte Zelthaut.

The Millennium Dome tent in the construction phase – Banana-shaped steel supports will bear the skin of the tent suspended from cables.

Für die Standfestigkeit dieses »fliegenden« Baus und seiner Dachhaut mußten mehr als 70 Kilometer extrastarken Stahlkabels verspannt werden.

More than 70 kilometres of extra-strong steel cable are necessary to ensure the stability of this »temporary« building.

Unten: Nördlich der Königlichen Sternwarte Greenwich, südlich der Isle of Dogs und weit westlich der City, genau auf der imaginären Achse des Null-Meridians befindet sich der Millennium Dome – für den ab dem 1.1.2000 zwölf bis fünfzehn Millionen britische und viele ausländische Besucher erwartet werden. Nächste Seiten: Millennium Dome bei Nacht.

Below: The Millennium Dome is located to the north of the Royal Observatory in Greenwich, to the south of the Isle of Dogs and far to the west of the city on the imaginary axis of the prime meridian. Up to 15 million British and foreign visitors are expected after 1.1.2000.
Following pages: The Millennium Dome at night.

2. Akt
Act 2

Architektur als Bühne – vergängliche Architektur
Architecture as stage – transitory architecture

Der Streit ist Jahrhunderte alt: Ist Architektur bildende oder nützliche Kunst? Ist sie Kunst? Der Konflikt wurde in den 80er Jahren sehr drastisch deutlich, als die artifiziellen Raumwunder einer postmodernen Museumsgeneration sich so darstellten, daß jeder Besucher fragen mußte: Exponat oder Architektur, was ist bitteschön mehr Kunst? | Diese am Ende unheilsame Konkurrenz ist hier nicht das Thema, doch die Aufgabe für Kunst, in diesem Falle die darstellende, eine angemessene Bühne zu bauen, ist reizvoll. Und die meisten der großen Architekten dieser Welt haben sich mit diesem Thema beschäftigt und dabei die Platzvorteile des temporären Bauens genutzt. | Wenig verwunderlich also, wenn Mario Botta dabei 1991 zur 700-Jahrfeier der Eidgenossenschaft eine Zeltkonstruktion wählte. Aber an dieser Stelle geht es nicht so sehr um das Zelt, sondern um die Zeichenhaftigkeit: silbern und kreisrund – ein Signal, das wandert und jeweils mit der wechselnden Umgebung eine neue Beziehung eingeht. »Bauen als Änderung des vorhandenen Gleichgewichts«, wie Botta sagt »das ist Architektur«. Und hier kann dies gleich mehrfach überprüft werden: in den Schweizer Bergen, am See, im Dialog mit einer Burg. »Vielleicht«, schreibt Botta zur Erläuterung weiter, »wird uns gerade die vergängliche Architektur, die nur im Moment dienen soll, behilflich sein, die Veränderungen, die wir erleben, zu deuten, zu kritisieren und zu schätzen!« | Die Kraft des »Provisoriums« vermag Dinge freizusetzen –

Die Kraft des »Provisoriums« vermag Dinge freizusetzen - in Kopf oder Seele, die fest gemauert in der Erde nicht so fließend herüberkommen.

The dispute is centuries old: Is architecture a fine or applied art? Is it art at all? In the 80's, the conflict became drastically clear when the artificial spatial miracles of a post-modern generation of museums were such that every visitor had to wonder whether the exhibit or the architecture itself was actually the work of art. | This finally unhealthy competition is not the topic here. Rather the task of creating a suitable stage for art, in this case the performing one, is a highly attractive enterprise. Most of the great architects of this world have involved themselves in this subject and made use of the advantages of space provided by temporary constructions. | It was therefore not so surprising when Mario Botta chose a tent construction for the 700th anniversary celebrations of the Swiss Confederation in 1991. But, at this point in our musings, the tent itself is less the focus of our thoughts than its symbolic nature: silver and round – a sign that travels and enters into a new relationship as its surroundings change their character. »Building as a change in the existing equilibrium«, as Botta said, »That is architecture.» And here, this can be demonstrated several times: in the Swiss mountains, at a

The power of the provisional is its ability to unleash those conceptions in the mind or the soul which, firmly embedded in immovable foundations, are difficult to put across in flowing terms.

in Kopf oder Seele, die fest gemauert in der Erde nicht so fließend herüberkommen. Berühmte Architekten zeigen, wie sie »fliegend« Doktrinen, Lehren, Scherze und Essenz ihrer Architektur transformieren. Das mag die archaische Zeichenhaftigkeit sein, aber auch die kinetische Veränderungsfähigkeit mobiler Bauten. Manchmal auch eine symbolische, pädagogische Arbeit, wie sie der Hamburger Architekt Andreas Heller an den fliegenden Bauten seiner Wanderausstellung »Sehnsucht« zeigt. | Unsere Beispiele haben eines gemeinsam: Sie sind Botschaften, von Bau- und Gestaltungsprofis und damit originelle Beiträge zur Stilgeschichte. Sie sind auch Gedankengebilde, die räumlich-plastisch werden oder einfach nur tolle Häuser, die demontabel sind!

lake, in a dialogue with a castle. »Perhaps« wrote Botta to clarify, »it is precisely such a transitory architecture, serving the particular moment, that can help us to interpret, criticise and appreciate the changes that we experience!« | The power of the provisional is its ability to unleash those conceptions in the mind or the soul which, firmly embedded in immovable foundations, are difficult to put across in flowing terms. Famous architects show how they transform, in passing, the doctrines, theses, jokes and the essence of their architecture. This may be archaic symbolism but it is also the capacity of mobile constructions for kinetic change -yet sometimes, as well, a symbolic, a pedagogic piece of work, a role demonstrated by the Hamburg architect Andreas Keller with the temporary buildings of his travelling exhibition »Sehnsucht» (Yearning). | Our examples have one thing in common: they are messages from the professionals in architecture and design and therefore original contributions to the history of style. They are also mental constructs which take on solid form or are simply wonderful-looking houses which can be taken to pieces!

Wandelndes Monument: ein Zelt zur 700-Jahrfeier der Schweiz

A changing monument: a tent for the 700th anniversary of Switzerland

Mario Botta, 1991

Vom 10. Januar des Jahres 1991 an wanderte ein Zelt des Tessiner Architekten Mario Botta durch die Eidgenossenschaft: beweglicher Feierort, 3.300 Kilogramm schwer, mit Wärmepumpen ausgerüstet und mit den 26 Kantonsbannern sowie der Schweizer Fahne geschmückt. 13 Stahlrohrwerke bilden in der Form eines Halbmondes mit einer Länge von gut 18 Metern das konstruktive Rückgrat. Die Schweiz ist ein Vier-Sprachen-Land, kein Vielvölkerstaat und dennoch multikulturell – das zeichenhafte Zelt sollte und konnte im Jahr 1991 ein Symbol der Einheit darstellen. Mario Botta: »Dieses Zelt soll mit seiner vergänglichen momentbezogenen Architekturform eine Deutung, Kritik, eine Wertschätzung, wie eine Einschätzung der Veränderungen unserer Zeit erleichtern.« Den Dia-

From 10 January 1991 onwards, a tent by the Ticino architect Mario Botta travelled through the Swiss Confederation, a mobile celebration weighing 3,300 kilograms, equipped with heating pumps and the banners of 26 cantons in addition to the Swiss flag itself. 13 steel-pipe structures form the backbone of the construction which is shaped like a half-moon and has a length of over 18 metres. Switzerland is a land of four languages, not a mixture of peoples but nevertheless multicultural. The tent was intended to be a symbol of unity, a function it fulfilled in 1991. According to Mario Botta, »This tent, with its transient architecture of the moment, is intended to facilitate interpretation, criticism, evaluation and estimation

log zwischen Architektur und Natur konnte Botta in sehr unterschiedlichen und immer wieder gewaltigen Landschaften der Schweiz führen: Die weiße Zeltkuppel paßt sich dabei den wechselnden Topographien von Berg und See perfekt an und ein, aber sie bleibt trotzdem auf unübersehbare Art und Weise präsent.

of the changes that are taking place in our times.« Botta was able to conduct this dialogue between architecture and nature in the very different but always magnificent countryside locations of Switzerland. The white cupola of the tent adapted itself perfectly to the changing topographies of mountain and lake, while still remaining eminently conspicuous.

Oben: Das Jubiläumszelt im Castelgrande in Bellinzona/Tessin – als sei es eine notwendige Ergänzung.
Rechts: Burggrundriß mit Zelt.

Top: The anniversary tent in the Castelgrande in Bellinzona/Ticino – with the appearance of a necessary adjunct.
Right: Ground plan of castle with tent.

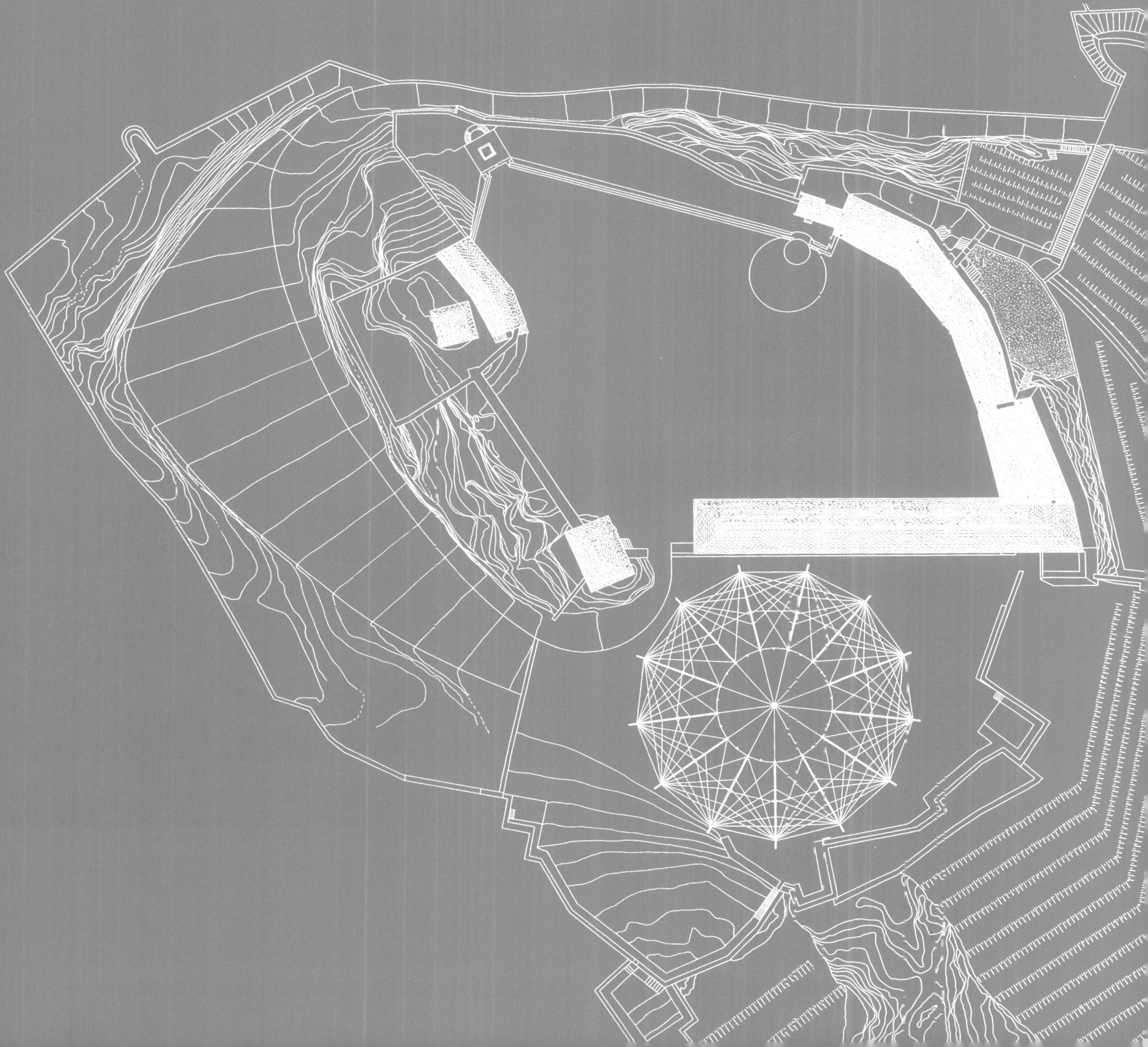

Bilder aus der Konstruktionsphase. Sie zeigen, wie die 13 Fachwerkträger für den Transport in jeweils drei Teile zerlegbar sind.

Pictures from the construction phase. They show how the 13 supporting beams can each be split up into three parts for transport.

Die fertig montierte Zeltkonstruktion wartet in Brunnen am See auf Festbesucher: »Bauen als Änderung des vorhandenen Gleichgewichts« (Mario Botta).

The completely constructed tent awaiting visitors in Brunnen am See. »Building as a change in the existing equilibrium« (Mario Botta).

Einige Daten:

Tragkonstruktion: Das Tragsystem wird aus 13 rund 18 Meter langen Stahl-Fachwerken gebildet, die kranzförmig und in einem Winkel von 45 Grad zum Boden geneigt angeordnet werden. Diese Stahlträger werden am Boden in Fundamentsockeln, am oberen Ende an einem Ring von rund 18 Metern Durchmesser, der ebenfalls mit runden Stahlprofilen ausgebildet ist, befestigt. Stahl-Fachwerk: Die »halbmondförmigen« Fachwerke lassen sich in je drei vorfabrizierte Elemente von ca. 6 Meter Länge und einem Gewicht von ca. 220 kg zerlegen Diese Elemente werden nur mit zwei Metallbolzen verbunden, die ebenfalls als Gelenk dienen. Die Montage ist somit sehr rasch und sicher. Oberer Ring: Der Ring mit einem rechteckigen Querschnitt von 1,5 x 2,9 Metern – wie die Fachwerke auch mit Rohrprofilen von ca. 150 mm Durchmesser ausgeführt – dient sowohl als obere Verankerung für die mittleren Fachwerke als auch zur Verankerung für die 26 Fahnenstangen und den »Laufsteg« für die Monteure der verschiedenen technischen Anlagen wie Scheinwerfer, Lautsprecher, Fernsehkameras usw.

Some data:

Load-bearing construction: The load-bearing system is composed of 13 steel lattice girders, each around 18 metres long, which are tilted at an angle of 45 degrees to the ground and arranged in a circle. These steel girders are anchored in the foundations and, at the top end, are attached to a ring with a diameter of around 18 metres, also made of shaped steel sections. Steel framework: The half-moonshaped lattice girders can each be taken apart into three prefabricated elements, each approximately 6 metres long and with a weight of around 220 kg. These elements are connected by only two metal bolts which also serve as articulated joints. Assembly is therefore extremely fast and reliable. Upper ring: The ring has a rectangular cross-section of 1.5 x 2.9 metres and, like the lattice girders, are made of shaped sections of pipe with a diameter of approximately 150 mm. The upper ring is using for anchoring the lattice girders in the middle and also the 26 flagpoles and the »gangway« for the fitters of the various items of technical equipment such as floodlights, loudspeakers, TV cameras etc.

下町唐座
下町唐座

Ort der Meditation: Kara Za Theater

Place of meditation: Kara Za theatre

Tadao Ando, Tokyo, 1988

Das bewegliche Theater war im Ursprung für die Avantgardetheatergruppe des Kara Joro mit dem Standort Asakusa entwickelt worden. Später wurde der Bau auch als Ausstellungshalle verwendet. Er ist 27 Meter hoch und mißt 20 Meter im Durchmesser. Der zwölfeckige Baukörper wird von einer Holzplankenfassade eingefaßt und durch ein rotes Zeltdach gekrönt. Ein Wiederaufbau an anderer Stelle ist innerhalb von 15 Tagen möglich. Mag es für die Augen des westlichen Beobachters sich vordergründig nur um einen Baukörper handeln, der mit einem behäbigen Wachturm verglichen werden kann, so ist es Ando doch auch hier wieder wie in seinen anderen Bauten gelungen, Botschaften fernöstlicher Lebensweise zu versenden. So wird beispielsweise das Theater über eine gebogene Brücke erreicht; Ando formuliert damit den Übergang von der realen Welt zum Reich der Illusionen. Der Transit von einer zur anderen Welt ist für Buddhisten ein Ort, der zur Meditation auffordert. Ein Bambuszaun – takeyarai – trennt die Kunstwelt des Theaters zusätzlich von ihrer natürlichen Umwelt – eine weitere symbolhafte Manifestation.

The mobile theatre had originally been developed for the avant-garde theatre group of the Kara Joro in Asakusa. Later, the construction was also used as an exhibition hall. It is 27 metres high with a diameter of 20 metres. The twelve-cornered structure is framed by a wooden-plank facade and crowned with a red tent roof. It can be rebuilt at another location within 15 days. To the eye of the western beholder, it may have something of the look of a watch-tower. But, as with his other buildings, Ando has again succeeded in conveying his message on the way of life in the Far East. The theatre is reached, for example, by a curved bridge, Ando's way of formulating the transition from the world of reality to the empire of illusion. For Buddhists the transition from one world to another is a place where meditation is called for. A bamboo fence – takeyarai – also separates the artificial world of the theatre from that of its natural surroundings – a further symbolic manifestation.

Links: Auch fliegende Bauten brauchen eine seriöse Gründung, deswegen dient hier eine Betonplatte als Fundament.
Unten: Schematische Grundriß-zeichnung des Theaters.

Left: Temporary buildings also need a serious foundation, in this case a concrete slab.
Below: Schematic drawing of the theatre's ground plan.

Fortführung des Aufbaus – wie er auf der linken Seite begonnen wurde. Noch fehlt die Holzplankenfassade (vgl. S. 67).

Continuation of construction – as begun on the left-hand page. The wooden-plank facade still has to be added (cf. p. 67).

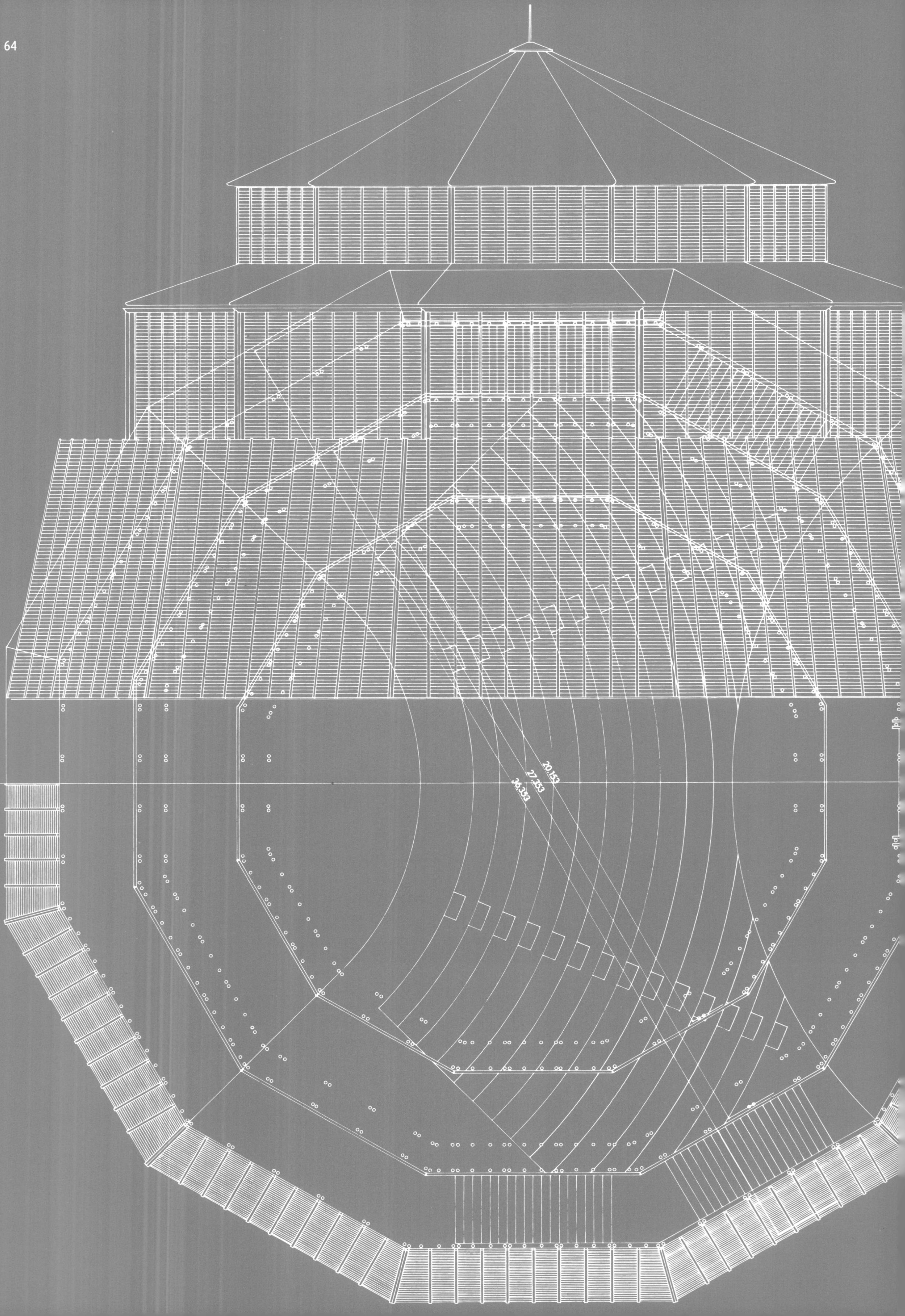

20.153
27.153
36.353

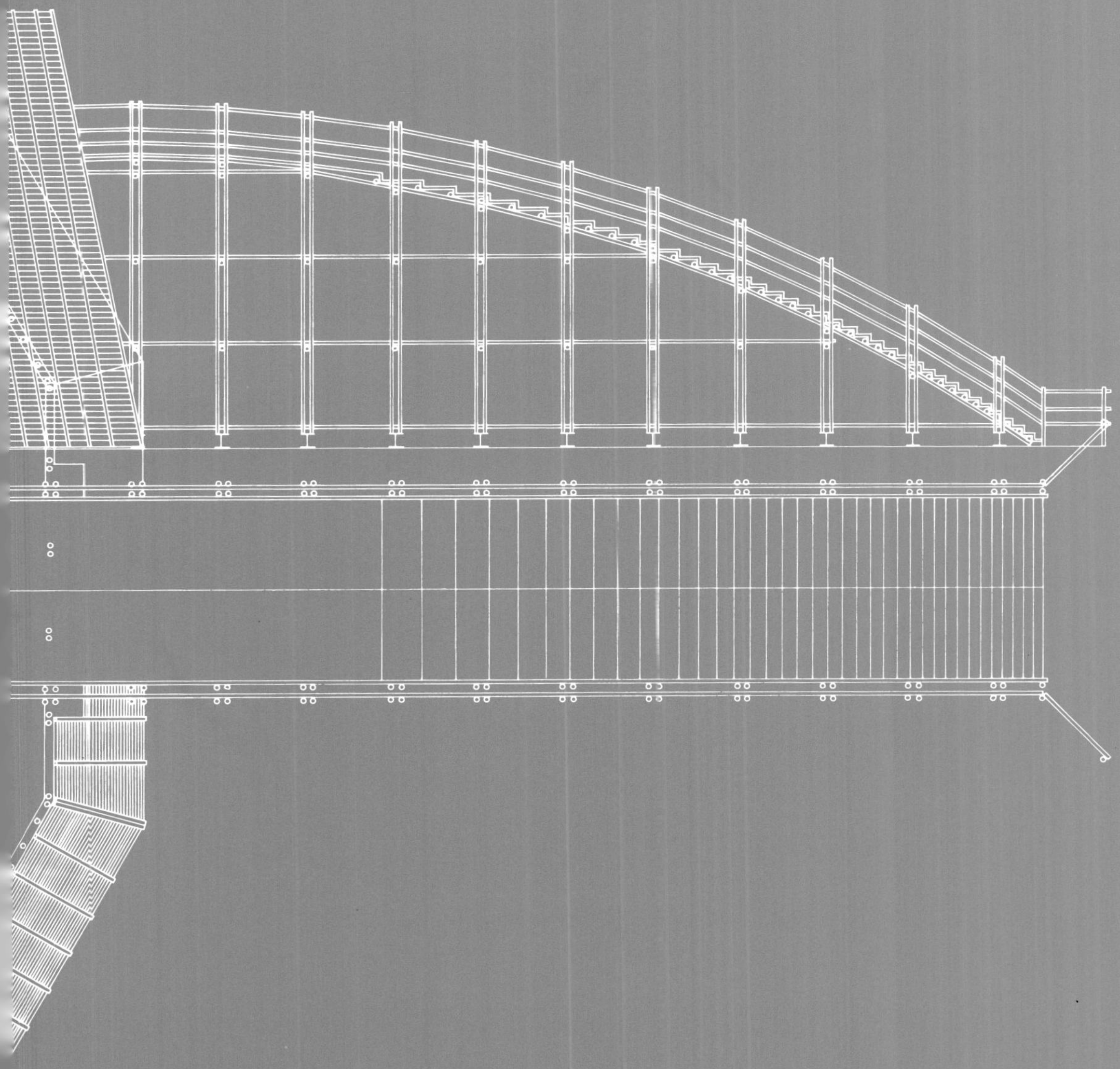

Zeichnung von Tadao Ando, die Aufriß (oben) und Grundriß in logischem Zusammenhang vereint.

Drawing by Tadao Ando in which the elevation (top) and ground plan are logically unified.

Links: Das Theater während
der Aufbauphase.
Rechts: Gesamtansicht mit
Außenhaut nach der Fertigstellung.

Left: The theatre during
the set-up phase.
Right: Overall view with outer
skin after completion.

»Ein Beruf ist das Rückgrat des Lebens.«
»Ein wenig Nachsicht, und die Kräfte verdoppeln sich.«
»Ich habe gelernt, allein zu leben. Da werden Kräfte frei.«
Ingrid van Bergen

Architektur gegen die Sucht: Sehnsucht

Architecture against addiction: Sehnsucht

Andreas Heller, Deutschland, 1998

Unter dem programmatischen Titel »Sehnsucht« hat die deutsche Zentrale für gesundheitliche Aufklärung die kongenialen Themen Sucht und Sehnsucht für eine Wanderausstellung aufbereiten lassen. Einerseits hatte ein praktikabler fliegender Bau zu entstehen, andererseits wollte das Team um den Designer Andreas Heller das Thema assoziativ wie auch architektonisch ansprechend umsetzen: mit »Stützen wie erstarrte Wellen, einer Muschel als Bauform umgeben von Wasser« (Pressetext). Sehnsucht nach Weite, Meer, Sonne, Luft wird mit Hilfe organischer Linienführung angesprochen. In der Ausstellung, per Video oder Vortrag, wird dann schnell verdeutlicht, daß aus jeder Sehnsucht Sucht werden kann, aber auch hinter jeder Sucht Sehnsucht steht. Das sanfte Äußere wird dann auch sehr brüsk mit einer »Suchtlandschaft« aus zickzack aufgestellten »Türen« konfrontiert. Spalten und Spione geben den Weg frei auf »klassische« Abhängigkeiten von Alkohol und Drogen oder auch auf Kauf-, Streit-, Arbeits- oder Magersucht. Die Wandermuschel des Andreas Heller macht deutlich: mit Architektur und Design kann man gesellschaftliche Probleme thematisieren.

Under the thematic title »Sehnsucht« (yearning), the deutsche Zentrale für gesundheitliche Aufklärung (German centre for health education), had the kindred themes of addiction and yearning prepared for a travelling exhibition. The aim was to create a practical temporary building, and a team headed by the designer Andreas Heller wanted to present these topics associatively and architecturally at the same time: »Supports like petrified waves, a mussel as a type of structure surrounded by water« (pressrelease text). Our yearning for the faraway, the sea, sun and air, is addressed with the help of flowing organic lines. In the exhibition itself, videos and presentations are used to illustrate how yearning can turn into an obsession and addiction. The gentle exterior is then very brusquely confronted by a »landscape of addiction«, made up of «doors» set up in a zig zag. Gaps and spy-holes open the view to people's »classical« dependency on alcohol and drugs or to their addiction to buying, arguing, working or dieting. The travelling mussel of Andreas Heller elucidates how architecture and design can represent themes relating to social problems.

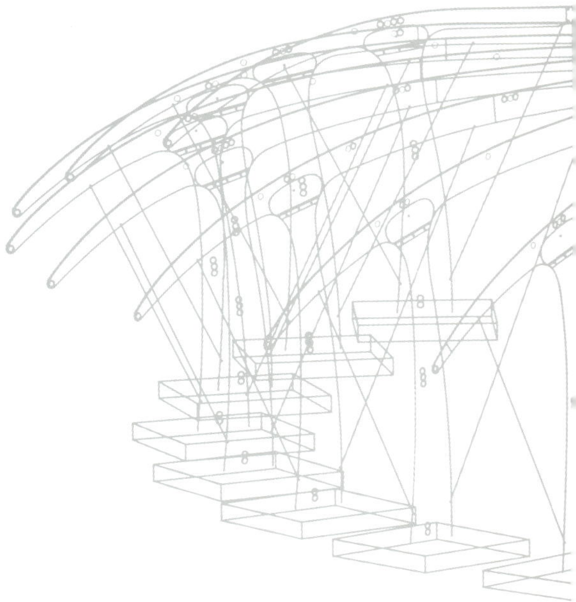

Aufbau des Pavillons vor den Hamburger Deichtorhallen: Flachbecken werden mit Wasser gefüllt und stabilisieren so den Stand der Stahlstützen. Die Transportcontainer gehören zum Gesamtkonzept und dienen als Rücken des muschelförmigen Pavillons.

The pavilion erected in front of the Hamburg Deichtorhalle: flat-bottomed basins are filled with water, thus stabilising the steel supports. The transport containers are part of the overall concept and act as the backbone of the mussel-shaped pavilion.

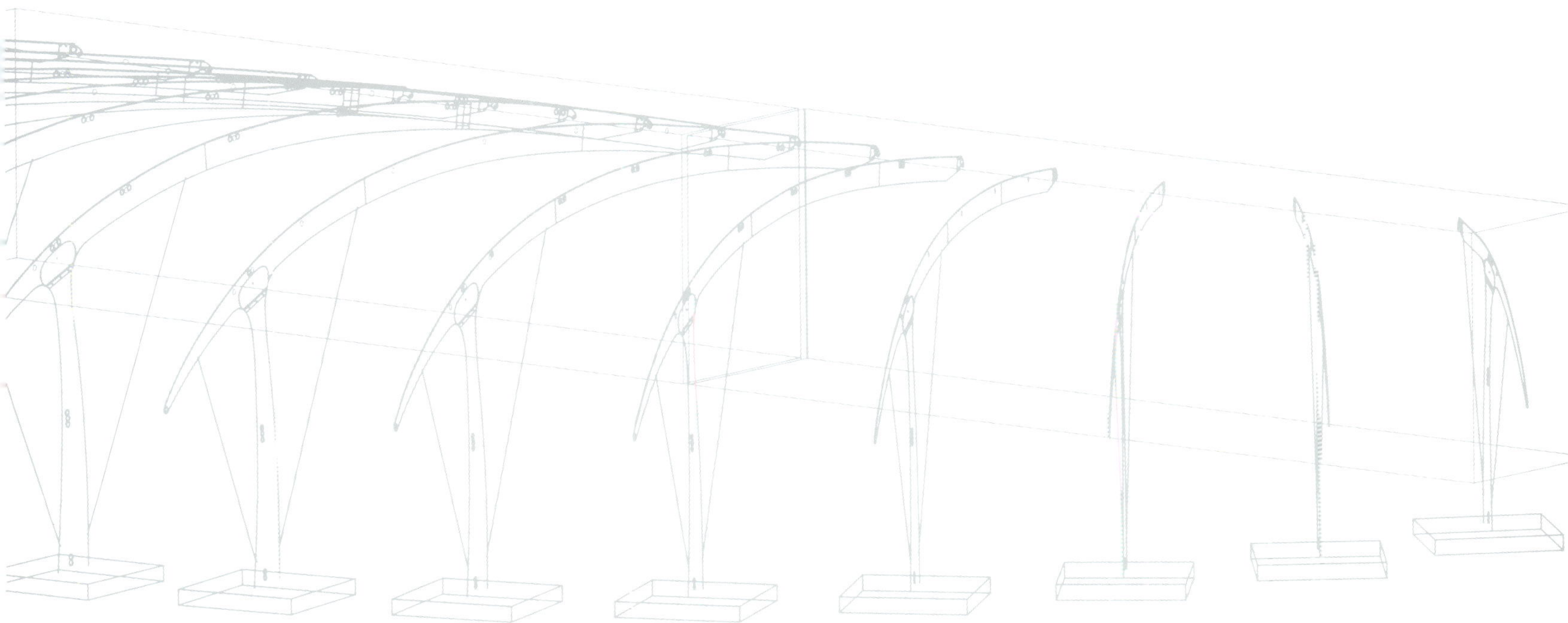

Perspektivische Schemaskizze der Tragkonstruktion; die Stützen werden so aufgestellt, daß der Pavillon einer Muschel ähnelt.

Schematic perspective of the load-bearing construction. The supports are erected so that the pavilion looks like a mussel.

Transluzente Lamellenpaneele bilden die Seitenwände des Bauwerks, ein symbolischer Hinweis darauf, daß der Inhalt - das Thema Sucht - für die gesamte Gesellschaft transparent gemacht werden soll (vgl. auch S. 68).

Translucent panels form the sidewalls of the structure - a symbolic reference to the topic of addiction, indicating that the topic is to be made transparent to the whole of society (cf. p. 68).

Vorherige Seiten: Aufbau der »Sehnsucht« am Kölner Dom. Es wurden Aufstellplätze favorisiert, an denen sich viele, vor allem junge Menschen aufhalten.
Unten: Der komplette Pavillon vor dem Hamburger Kunstzentrum »Deichtorhallen«, in der Nähe des Hauptbahnhofs.

Previous pages: »Sehnsucht« erected at the cathedral in Cologne. Locations were preferred where a lot of young people were often to be found.
Below: The complete pavilion in front of the Hamburg Kunstzentrum »Deichtorhallen«, near the central station.

Links: Aufbau in Frankfurt.
Aus der Luft gesehen wird die Muschelform besonders deutlich.
Rechts: Die Aluminiumbinder der Konstruktion ragen wie Zacken aus der Konstruktion heraus.

Left: Set up in Frankfurt. Seen from the air, the mussel shape is especially apparent
Right: The aluminium trusses of the construction protrude from the construction like prongs.

Dino Rosso contra Captain Isy: Entertainment Pavillon

Dino Rosso versus Captain Isy: a pavilion of entertainment

Matteo Thun, Kirchhellen, 1993

Der Südtiroler Designer und Architekt Matteo Thun hat mit seiner Entertainment-Skulptur im Bavaria-Filmpark (Kirchhellen, Westfalen) eine Nische zwischen Popkultur, Theaterbau und Kommerzialität gekonnt besetzt. Die Skulptur ist mehrteilig: Ein rot bespannter »Drachenleib«, die Phantasy-Figur Dino Rosso, und darüber die fliegende Schildkröte Captain Isy bilden die Ouvertüre. Eine 22 Meter hohe Sil-

With his entertainment sculpture in the Bavarian Filmpark (Kirchhellen, Westphalia), the south-Tyrolean designer and architect Matteo Thun has occupied a niche between pop culture, theatre construction and commercialism. The sculpture has several parts. A red dragon's torso, the fantasy figure Dino Rosso and, above this, the flying tortoise, Cap-

berkugel, die an eine Raumkapsel gemahnt, und ein »Shop Container« schließen sich an. In der silbernen Raumschiffkuppel werden die Besucher von einem multimedialen Spektakel empfangen, das Robert Wilson inszeniert hat. In einer Multimedia-Show wird die Geschichte von Captain Isy, der von einem Lichtjahre entfernten Planeten kam, erzählt – mit der Hardware einer Unterhaltungselektronik-Firma, die diesen Pavillon gesponsert hat. Denn das ist das Anliegen: in märchenhafter Szene, scheinbar aller Realität entrückt, die Leistungsfähigkeit von elektronischem Fortschritt aufzuzeigen.

tain Isy, form the overture, and joined to them, a 22 metre-high silver ball, reminiscent of a space capsule, and a »shop container«. In the silver spaceship cupola, visitors are welcomed by a multi-media spectacle, stage-managed by Robert Wilson. In a multi-media show, the story of Captain Isy who comes from a planet light-years away is told with the hardware of an electronics entertainment company which has sponsored the pavilion. And this is in fact the purpose of the pavilion – to illustrate the capabilities of electronic progress in a fairytale manner, apparently beyond the bounds of reality.

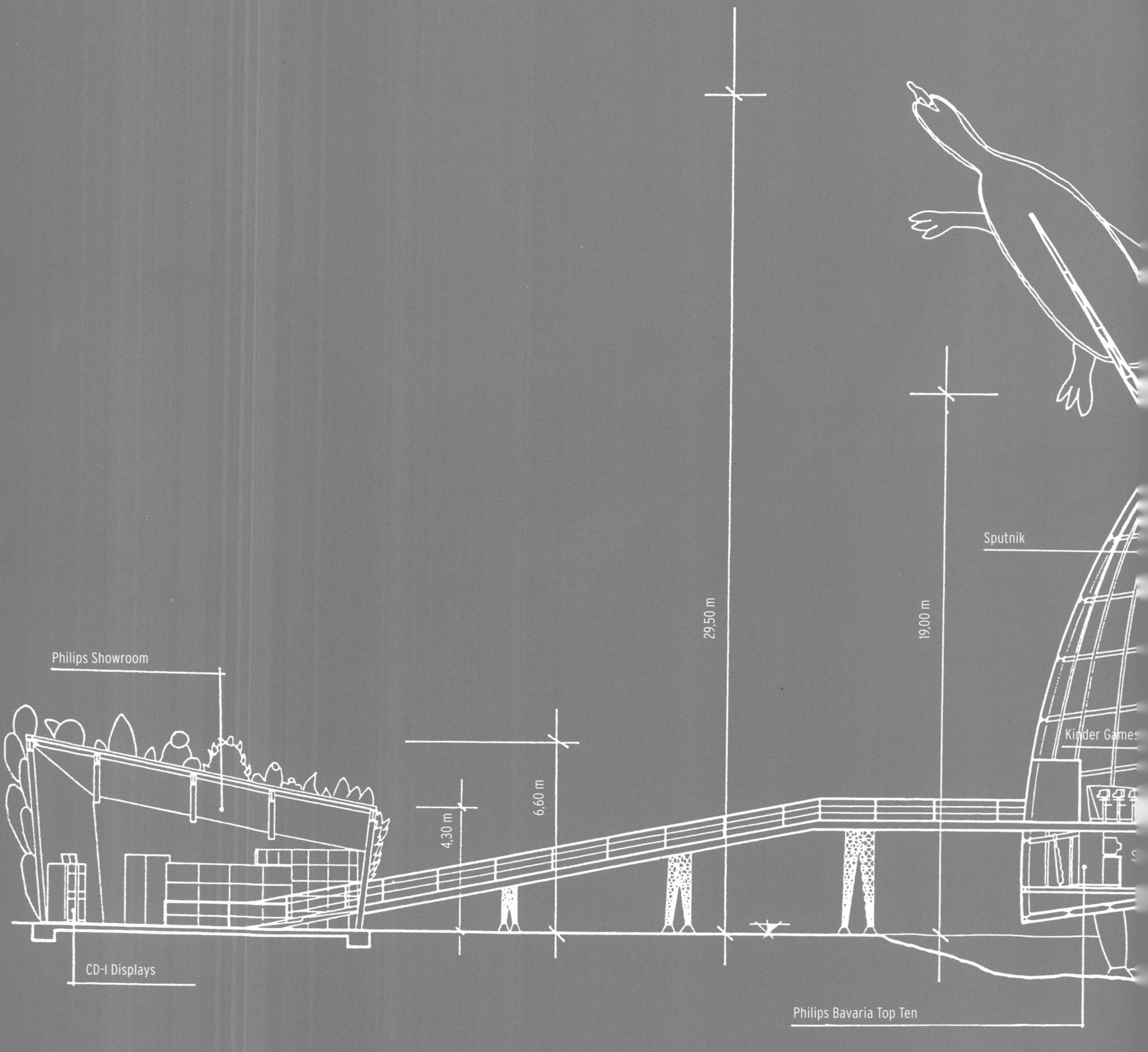

Sputnik
29,50 m
19,00 m
Philips Showroom
Kinder Games
6,60 m
4,30 m
CD-I Displays
Philips Bavaria Top Ten

Einige Daten:

Grundgerüst aus Stahl ca. 140 Tonnen; Höhe des Sputniks: 18 m, Durchmesser 18 m, Länge Dinosaurier 18 m; Membrane aus PVC-Polyester mit HT-Fluorpolymertopcoat und Trägergewebe aus PES, schwer entflammbar; Gefertigt als Luftkissen, gefüllt mit 240 Pascal Druck Beleuchtung: 7.850 Halogenkaltlichtlampen, einzeln steuerbar über Computeranlage.

Some data:

Basic frame made of steel, approx. 140 metric tons. Height of the sputnik, 18 m, diameter 18 m. Dinosaur 18 m long made of PVC with HT fluoro-polymer top coat and fabric made of PES, flame-retardant. Made as an air cushion, inflated with a pressure of 250 pascals. Illumination: 7,850 halogen coldlight lamps, individually controllable by computer system.

Eine der Phantasyfiguren, der ignorante Dino Rosso (vgl. auch S. 76 bis 79), versucht, in die Welt der digitalen Spiele einzudringen. Er hat keine Chance – die großen und kleinen Spieler haben auf dem Bildschirm ihren eigenen Kosmos gefunden, von dem Captain Isy, die Schildkröte, erzählt.

One of the fantasy figures, the ignorant Dino Rosso (cf. p. 76 to 79), tries to penetrate the world of digital games. He doesn't have a chance – small and large players havefound their own cosmos on the screen and Captain Isy, the tortoise, tells the story.

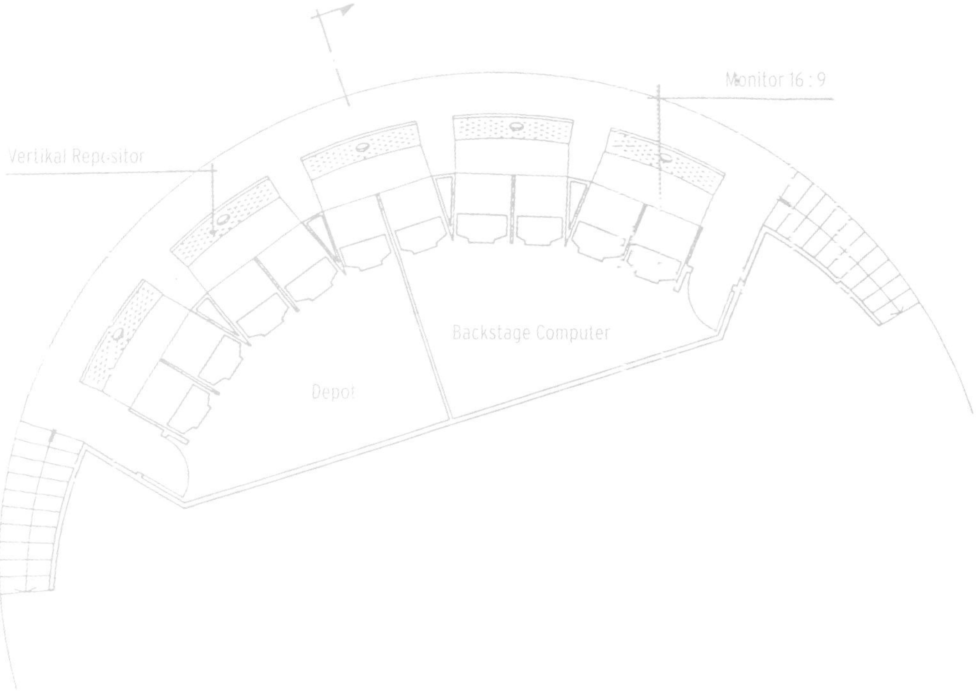

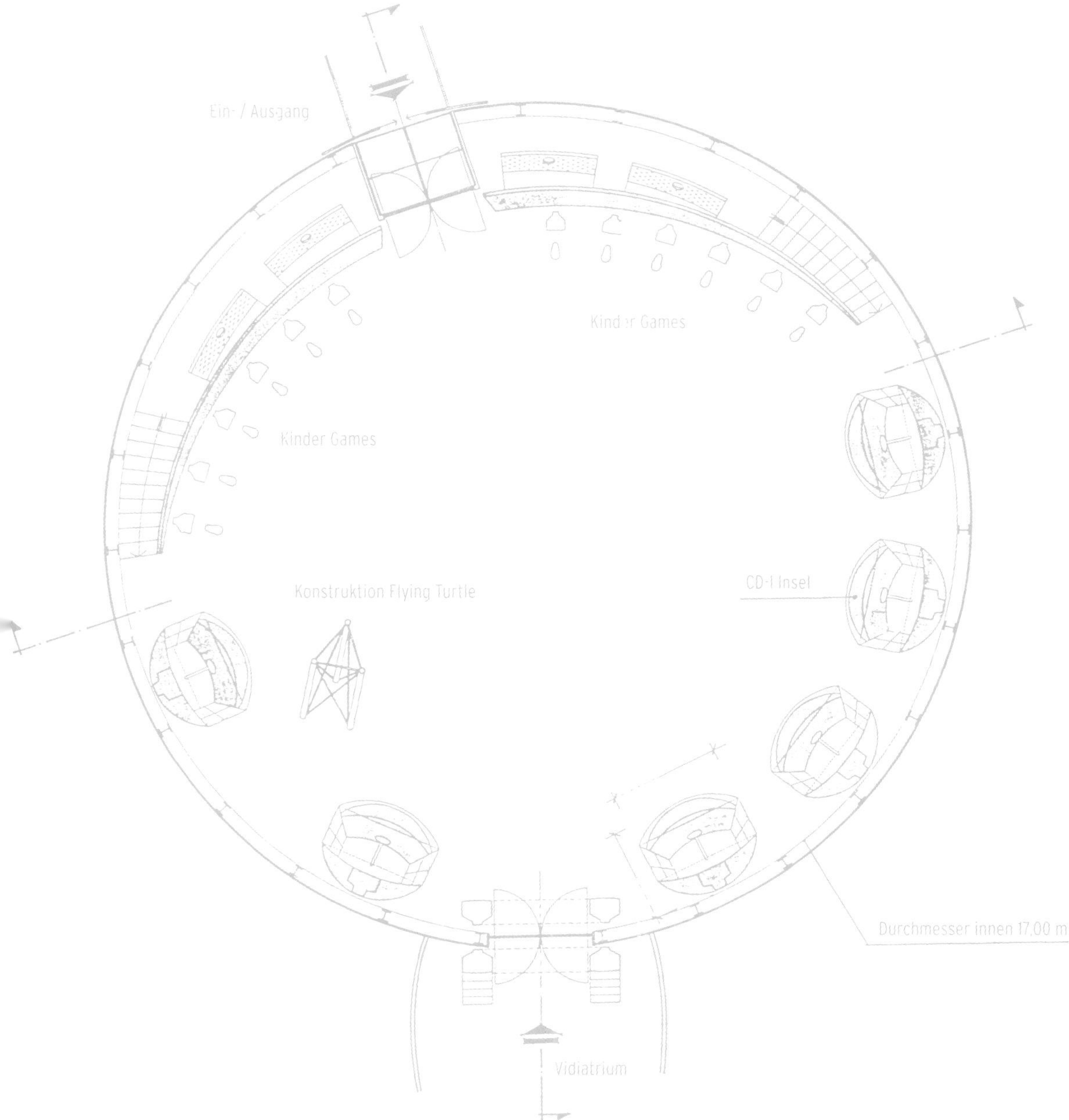

Oben: Grundriß Untergeschoß des Pavillons.
Links: Grundriß Hauptebene mit Kinderspielstationen und CD-I (CD-interaktiv)-Kapseln.

Above: Ground plan of the pavilion's basement.
Left: Ground plan of the main level with children's play-stations and CD-I (CD interactive) capsules.

Links: Die aufragende Schwanzspitze von Dino Rosso.
Unten: Die Schildkröte Captain Isy thront über allem.
Rechts: Neuentwickelte »CD-I-Insel« für das interaktive Computerspiel, aufgebaut im silbernen Philips-Pavillon.

Left: The prominent tip of Dino Rosso's tail.
Below: Captain Isy, the tortoise, sits enthroned above everything.
Right: Newly developed »CD-I-island« for interactive computer games, set up in the silver Philips pavilion.

TOP 10
PHILIPS

DANIEL LIBESKIND
BEYOND THE WALL
6.9 – 23.11 1997
The exhibition is composed of architectural models and drawings as well as their extension into the concrete space they open to the public. This particular exhibition represents the **search for architecture** and is a microcosm of ideas and thoughts. It is the intention of the exhibition design that the public co-participate in a scheme by following an imaginative and non-linear path in order to experience 'the other side', 'the substance' of hope and the proof of what remains invisible in

Kafkaesker Irrgarten: Beyond the wall 26,36°

A Kafkaesque maze: Beyond the wall 26,36 °

Daniel Libeskind, Rotterdam, 1997

Die Hauptausstellungshalle des NAi (Nederlands Architectuurinstituut) in Rotterdam ist groß und hoch; eine ideale Hülle für eine außergewöhnliche Installation: 50.000 Schrauben halten eine Landschaft aus Holz, Stahl und Stahlblech zusammen, deren Fläche insgesamt 1.800 Quadratmeter ergeben. Die Ausstellung hat etwa zwei Millionen Mark gekostet. Es ist so, als habe der Architekt Daniel Libeskind im Herbst 1997 ein Gebirge aus metallischen Schluchten und Steilwänden komponieren wollen. In Wahrheit ist es eine Bühne: Die Nebendarsteller hier sind Modelle und auch Zeichnungen seiner Architekturprojekte – sie sind beiläufig, das heißt selbstverständlich und in guter Augenhöhe integriert. Alles andere ist nicht selbstverständlich in diesem Labyrinth der spiralförmigen Wege, zwischen den galvanisierten Stahlplatten, die spitz und schräg herumstehen.

The main exhibition hall of the NAi (Nederlands Architektuur Instituut) in Rotterdam is wide and high, an ideal housing for an unusual installation: 50,000 screws hold together a landscape of wood steel and metal sheeting, which together form a total surface area of 1,800 square metres. The exhibition constructed in the autumn of 1997 cost around two million marks. It is as if the architect, Daniel Libeskind, wanted to compose a mountain with metal gorges and steel walls. In reality, it is a stage. The supporting actors here are models and drawings of his architectural projects, casually integrated in the setting and, of course, at eye level. But there is no »of course« about anything else in this labyrinth of spiral pathways between galvanised steel plates, both pointed and slanting.

Libeskind-Ausstellung im Rotterdamer NAi: Entwurf für die Erweiterung des Londoner Victoria & Albert-Museums.

Libeskind exhibition in the NAi, Rotterdam: a design for the extension to the Victoria & Albert Museum in London.

Rechts: Die Ausstellung als Irrgarten - mit Ausweg.
Nächste Seiten: Die Ausstellungsarchitektur als Wiederholung der originalen Entwurfsmotive des Daniel Libeskind.

Right: Exhibition and maze - with an exit.
Next pages: The exhibition architecture as a repetition of the original design motifs of Daniel Libeskind.

Aber diese Platten sind die Hauptdarsteller, denn schnell begreift der Besucher, daß die Installation nichts anderes als ein 1 : 1 - Modell der Libeskindschen Baukünste ist. Dieser Architekt denkt stets kafkaesk und verwirrt gern seine Besucher oder sogar seine Bauherren. Er läßt aber immer Hoffnung auf einen Ausweg zu. So auch hier, in dieser verwirrenden Ausstellung, in der sich dennoch niemand verlaufen hat. Die Parallelen zwischen seinen »wirklichen« Häusern, so einem Erweiterungsbau an das Londoner Victoria & Albert Museum, und der Ausstellungsbühne für seine Architektur zeigen sich auf Schritt und Tritt. Säulenfrei und ohne tragendes Gerüst drehen und schrauben sich seine Wände in die Luft, ob mobil in der Ausstellung, oder in für die Ewigkeit gegossenen Beton im Museumsbau.

But it is these plates which are the protagonists as the visitor quickly understands that the installation is nothing other than a 1 to 1 model of Libeskind's architecture. This architect's mode of thought is always Kafkaesque and he likes to confuse his visitors and even his clients. But he always leaves room for hoping there is a way out. This confusing exhibition is no different but no-one has yet lost their way. The parallels between his »real« buildings, such as the extension to the Victoria & Albert Museum in London, and the exhibition stage for his architecture are apparent at every step. Without any columns and without a load-bearing framework, the walls twist and turn in the air, whether they are mobile in the exhibition or made of concrete cast for eternity in the museum building.

1.800 Quadratmeter Stahlblech bilden eine ungewöhnliche Ausstellungslandschaft, die einen weit präziseren Einblick in die Arbeit des Architekten bietet als aufgestellte Modelle und aufgehängte Pläne.

1,800 square metres of steel sheet create an unusual exhibition landscape which provides a much more precise insight into the work of the architect than models and plans on the walls.

3. Akt
Act 3

Stage Architecture: Zwischen Happening und multimedialer Performance

Stage architecture: between happening and multimedia performance

Organisch, fließend: Voodoo Lounge, Rolling Stones

Kommerziell: Popmart, U2

Explosiv: Division Bell, Pink Floyd

Technoid: Dance into the Light, Phil Collins

Barock: Bridges to Babylon, Rolling Stones

Organic and flowing: Voodoo Lounge, Rolling Stones

Commercial: Popmart, U2

Explosive: Division Bell, Pink Floyd

Technoid: Dance into the Light, Phil Collins

Baroque: Bridges to Babylon, Rolling Stones

Im griechischen Drama markiert meist im 3. Akt die Peripetie ein plötzliches Umschlagen, eine unerwartete Wendung; Peripetie ist auch der Höhepunkt einer dramatischen Entwicklung. Die multimediale Performance, die zum Ruhme und auch zum Profit von Popstars auf ihren Tourneen inszeniert wird, ist für die Kultur der mobilen Bühnen so etwas wie ein dramatischer Höhepunkt. | Seit 1965 mit den Beatles die Ära der Stadionkonzerte begann, mußten sich die Bühnenarchitekten auf immer größere Arenen und Bühnen einstellen. So natürlich auch der Londoner Architekt Mark Fisher, der vor 25 Jahren mit Bühnenkulissen für Musicals wie »Jesus Christ Superstar« and »The Rocky Horror Picture Show« begann und dessen Durchbruch als Stage Designer das martialische Szenario von »The Wall« 1990 für Pink Floyd in historischer Berliner Mauer-Landschaft markierte. Fishers Hauptwerk liegt in den 90er Jahren. Ein neuer Gigantismus bei Konstruktion und Durchführung ist entstanden. Aber das hilft auch dem Zuschauer in der

Die multimediale Performance, die zum Ruhme und auch zum Profit von Popstars auf ihren Tourneen inszeniert wird, ist für die Kultur der mobilen Bühnen so etwas wie ein dramatischer Höhepunkt.

In Greek drama, the peripeteia, usually in the 3rd act, marks a sudden reversal of circumstances, an unexpected turn of events. Peripeteia is also the climax of a dramatic development. The multimedia performance which is stage managed for the fame and also the profit of pop stars on their tours is thus something like a dramatic climax for the culture of mobile stages. | Since 1965 when the era of stadium concerts began with the Beatles, stage architects have had to get used to bigger and bigger arenas and stages. The London architect, Mark Fisher, for example, who began 25 years ago with the stage scenery for musicals such as »Jesus Christ Superstar« and »The Rocky Horror Picture Show« and saw his breakthrough as a Stage Designer for the martial setting of »The Wall« for Pink Floyd in 1990 against the historical walled landscape of Berlin. Fisher's main work was in the 90's. A new giantism in construction and realisation was created. But this also helps the people in the thousandth row to half-way follow the show.

tausendsten Reihe, die Show noch halbwegs verfolgen zu können. | Solche Spektakel entwirft man nicht mehr auf Papier und mit Pappe, sondern digital bewegt: »Am Ende ist alles möglich, es beginnt bei einer leeren Bühne, minimalistisch, japanisch, aber wir können Ihnen auch eine barocke Kathedrale aufbauen«, wie Fisher seinen Arbeitsauftrag beschreibt. Die Stars sorgen dafür, daß sich über die Architektur des Modernisten Fisher weitere bunte Schichten legen. Bühnen für die Rolling Stones wirken mit ihren Rampen und Lampions wie riesige Fahrgeschäfte auf dem Münchner Oktoberfest. Pink Floyds »Division Bell« von 1994 ist eine wahre Rockshow-Inszenierung, die mit Licht und Feuer die Nacht zum Tage werden läßt. | Längst sind die Live-Konzerte im Stadion zu einem virtuellen Übertragungsmeisterwerk per Bildschirm und elektro-akustischer Verstärkung geworden: Stage Design im Schlagschatten von Popsendern wie MTV und der »Softdroge« Coca Cola als globale Botschaft westlicher Gesellschaften. Alle zusammen inszenieren einen riesigen bunten Videoclip, in dem Gebautes mit Illusionärem, die Performances der Stars mit Licht und Musik verschmelzen. Und die Zuschauer switchen ob des Superangebots für die Augen herum wie beim Zapping vor dem Puschenkino.

Such spectacles are no longer designed on paper and with cardboard models but are digital and animated. »In the end, everything is possible. It begins with an empty stage, minimalist, Japanese, but we can also build you a baroque cathedral«, as Fisher describes his task. The stars ensure that additional colourful layers are arranged, on top of the architecture of Fisher, the modernist. Stages for the Rolling Stones, with their ramps and lampions, look like enormous rides at the Oktoberfest in Munich. Pink Floyd's »Division Bell« of 1994 is a true rock-show stage setting, transforming night into day with its light beams and fire. | Live concerts in stadiums have long since become virtual masterpieces transmitted by screens and electro-acoustic amplification – stage design in the shadow of pop stations such as MTV and the »soft-drug« Coca Cola as a global message of western societies. All these together provide the setting for a huge, multi-coloured video clip, in which the constructed merges with the illusory and the performances of the stars with the light and the music. And the audience switches from one superlative to the next – as a treat for the eyes, like zapping between stations on the box in our living rooms.

The multimedia performance which is stage managed for the fame and also the profit of pop stars on their tours is thus something like a dramatic climax for the culture of mobile stages.

Organisch, fließend: Voodoo Lounge, Rolling Stones

Organic and flowing: Voodoo Lounge, Rolling Stones

Mark Fisher und Jonathan Park, 1994

Die Bühnen der beiden Mega-Tourneen der Rolling Stones, »Voodoo Lounge« 1994 und »Steel Wheels« 1989, wurden von sehr langen Laufstegen flankiert. Mick Jagger rennt eben gern beim Singen. Im Gegensatz zur »Steel Wheels«-Tour, die irgendwo zwischen »Post-Blade Runner, Grunge und Science Fiction« (Fisher) angelegt war, sollte hier das Bühnenbild organischer und fließender wirken. Tatsächlich wird die alles beherrschende Videowand von gekurvten und gerundeten Baukörpern eingerahmt. Mark Fishers architektonische Heimat ist die Moderne: »Bei mir ist Stahl Stahl, Alu ist Alu!« Aber zu seiner Lieblings-Moderne gehören nicht nur die Klassiker, sondern auch große Expressionisten wie der Katalane Antonio Gaudi oder der deutsche Hans Scharoun. Voodoo Lounge läßt diese Vergangenheit anklingen … .

The stages of the two mega-tours of the Rolling Stones, »Voodoo Lounge« in 1994 and »Steel Wheels« in 1989, were flanked by very long catwalks; Mick Jagger likes to run when he sings. In contrast to the »Steel Wheels« tour, which was somewhere between »post-Blade Runner grunge and science fiction« (Fisher), the stage scenery here was to have a more organic and flowing effect. The dominant video screen is framed by curved and rounded elements. Mark Fisher's architectural homeland is the modern: »For me, steel is steel, aluminium is aluminium!« But his favourite modern architecture includes not only that of the classicists but also of the great expressionists such as the Catalonian Antonio Gaudi or the German Hans Scharoun. Voodoo Lounge relives this past … .

Während der Show, so war es angestrebt und wurde es auch erreicht, sollte sich der technoide Anblick bei Tag in einen »verwirrenden Schrein der Konsumgüter, in ein surreales Tableau alltäglicher Gegenstände« (Mark Fisher) verwandeln.

During the show, the aim and the achievement was to transform the technoid view by day into a »chaotic shrine to consumer goods, into a surreal tableau of everyday objects« (Mark Fisher).

Oben: Voodoo-Lounge –
Live-Eindrücke aus der Show.
Nächste Seiten: Ikonen aus vielen Zeitepochen wachen über Mick & Co: unter anderem eine Hindu-Göttin, die Jungfrau Maria und Elvis.

Top: Voodoo Lounge –
Live impressions from the show.
Following pages: Icons from several eras watch over Mick and his friends: a Hindu goddess, the Virgin Mary and Elvis.

Kommerziell: Popmart, U2

Commercial: Popmart, U2

Mark Fisher und Willie Williams, 1997

Es ist das Schlüsselthema in der Pop-Welt: Konsum und Kommerz. Der Popmarkt der Gruppe U2 schmückt sich mit symbolischen Einkaufskörben und einem riesigen Bogen, dessen Herkunft aus der Welt der Fleischklopsbrater unverkennbar ist. Beim »Popmart« von U2 bricht Fisher gleich reihenweise Rekorde – mit der bis dahin größten installierten Vierfarb-Videoleinwand mit 700 Quadratmetern und einem demontablen Triumphbogen von 30 Metern Höhe, so daß ein Hubschrauber darunter durchfliegen könnte. »Popmart« ist aber auch der klassische Beweis dafür, daß bei mobilen Bühnen nicht nur das »schöne« Design zählt, sondern auch Praktikabilität und Mobilität. Die gesamte Stahlkonstruktion, die Glasfiber-Fassadenelemente und auch der Video-Bildschirm sind modular entworfen worden, so daß sie gefahrlos, schnell und präzise auf Trucks ver-

It is the key topic of the pop world: consumption and commerce. The Popmart of the group U2 adorns itself with symbolic shopping baskets and a huge arch whose origins in the world of the cheap hamburger are unmistakable. Fisher breaks a whole series of records with his »Popmart« of U2 – the largest four-colour video screen of 700 square metres ever installed and a removable triumphal arch, 30 metres high, under which a helicopter could fly. »Popmart«, however, is also classical proof that not only an »attractive« design counts with mobile stages but also their practicability and mobility. The whole steel construction, the glass-fibre facade elements and the video screen have a modular design so that they can be loaded onto trucks safely, quickly and precisely. Special cranes and transportable motors help during

laden werden können. Spezialkräne und transportable Motoren helfen bei Ab- und Aufbau. »Popmart« mußte deutschen und amerikanischen Vorschriften entsprechen und Windgeschwindigkeiten bis zu 120 km/h widerstehen. Sogar kalifornische Erdbebenvorschriften mußten erfüllt werden. Für die entsprechende Standfestigkeit sorgten unter anderem Stahlfundamentwannen, die mit Wasser gefüllt wurden.

erecting and dismantling work. »Popmart« had to comply with German and American regulations and withstand wind speeds of up to 120 kph. Even Californian earthquake regulations had to be complied with. Steel-foundation basins filled with water helped to keep the structure stable.

Allen Entwürfen Mark Fishers ist eigen, daß sie von der ersten Skizze (vgl. S. 106/107) bis zur Realisierung ihren ursprünglichen Charakter nicht mehr verändern. Zu den Motiven Bogen und Einkaufskorb gesellte sich auf Wunsch von U2 noch eine Zitrone: als zusätzliche Bühne.

A feature of all Mark Fisher's designs is that they do not change their character, from the first sketch (cf. p. 106/107) to actual construction. In addition to the motifs of the arch and the shopping baskets, U2 also wanted a lemon as an additional stage.

Der 30 Meter hohe Bogen wurde mit gelben Paneelen aus Aluminium und Glasfiber-Kunststoff verkleidet. Die Video-Leinwand ist 700 Quadratmeter groß. Wenn sie nicht benutzt wird, wirkt sie halbtransparent, weil die einzelnen Pixel auf Abstand montiert sind.

The 30 metre-high arch was covered with yellow panels made of aluminium and glass-fibre plastic. The video screen is 700 square metres in size. When it is not being used, it looks semi-transparent because the individual pixels are separate from each other.

Was am Ende, trotz aller Größe, die Leichtigkeit einer Theaterkulisse haben soll, ist im Falle der Leinwand 19 Meter hoch und besteht aus belastbaren Materialien wie zum Beispiel Stahl. Zum Aufbau werden Spezialkräne benötigt, die Video-Leinwand wird von aufgehängten Motoren hochgezogen.

What, in the end, displayed the lightness of a theatre stage setting is, in the case of the screen, 19 m high and consists of a stress-resistant materials such as steel. Special cranes are needed to erect it and the video screen is hoisted by suspended motors.

Eine fahrbare, überdimensionale Zitrone wird im Laufe der Show zur zusätzlichen Bühne, zum neuen überraschenden Element der Inszenierung – eine Änderung von Spielort und Perspektive für die Zuschauer.

A transportable, overdimensional lemon turns into an additional stage during the show; an element of surprise in the setting – a change of location and perspective for the audience.

Explosiv: Division Bell, Pink Floyd

Explosive: Division Bell, Pink Floyd

Mark Fisher, 1994

Gerade mit den Entwürfen für Pink Floyds »Division Bell« 1994 wird deutlich, daß Rockshow-Inszenierungen für die Nacht angelegt werden, mit Lichtdomen, Feuerwerk, künstlicher Lava bis zur Simulation von Mini-Atomexplosionen. Eine Reise ins Licht und der nachhaltige Beweis dafür, daß Stage Architecture multidimensionaler als die gute alte Bühnenarchitektur einer Zauberflöteninszenierung ist.

The designs for Pink Floyd's »Division Bell« 1994 illustrate that rock-show productions are created for the night – with light cupolas, fireworks, artificial lava and even the simulation of mini atomic bombs. A journey into light and lasting proof that stage architecture is more multi-dimensional than the good old stage architecture associated with a production of The Magic Flute.

Die Bühne für die Division-Bell-Tour entlarvt sich bei Tage als nüchterne, funktionale Konstruktion. Die Großform erinnert an das Schutzdach so mancher Kurkonzertbühnen.

By day, the stage for the Division Bell tour reveals itself as a sober, functional construction whose shape is reminiscent of the protective roof seen over many concert stages.

Wie von einem anderen Stern wirkt das verzauberte Nachtgesicht der Bühne, wenn die Show vor der runden Leinwand tobt.

The enchanted night-time face of the stage looks like it comes from another star when the show rages in front of the projection screen.

Laserlicht und Feuerwerk sorgen dann endgültig für die visuelle Auflösung einer begrenzten, lokalisierten Architektur – die Show wird Gesamtkunstwerk, Vision, virtuelle Architektur.

Laser lights and fireworks finally ensure the visual break-up of a limited, localised architecture. The show becomes an overall work of art, a vision of virtual architecture.

Technoid: Dance into the Light, Phil Collins

Technoid: Dance into the Light, Phil Collins

Mark Fisher, 1997

Eine typische Indoor-Arbeit von Mark Fisher ist die »Dance into the Light Tour« für den Rockbarden Phil Collins. Sie kombiniert modernste Technik mit abenteuerlicher Raumkunst. Phil Collins singt und spielt auf einer künstlichen Insel mitten im Menschenmeer seiner Zuhörer. Über ihm schwebt eine stählerne Kuppel, die sich wie ein Schirm öffnen läßt. Je nach Stellung der einzelnen Panele wirkt die Bühneninstallation wie ein UFO oder ein U-Boot. Die perfekte Bewegung des Öffnens und Schließens ist wirkungsvoller als jede Dekoration – Maschinenästhetik und Architektur. »Neueste Technologie beeinflußt, beeindruckt mich«, kommentiert Fisher seinen eigenen Stil, »und ich will Grenzen überschreiten!«

The »Dance into the Light Tour« for the rock-poet, Phil Collins, is a typical piece of indoor work by Mark Fisher. It combines the latest technology with adventurous spatial art. Phil Collins sings and plays on an artificial island in the middle of a sea of listeners. Above him hovers a steel cupola which can be opened like an umbrella. Depending on the position of the single panels, the stage installation can look like a UFO or a submarine. The perfect movement during opening and closing is more effective than any decoration – a kind of mechanical aesthetics and architecture. »The latest technology influences and impresses me«, remarks Fisher on his personal style, »and I want to go beyond the limits!«.

Viele Bühnenentwürfe von Mark Fisher sind auf Flugreisen entstanden: Mit wenigen Strichen werden Raum und Struktur skizziert - wie hier für Phil Collins Indoor Tour »Into the Light«.

Many stage designs by Mark Fisher originated on plane journeys. The space and the structure are sketched with a few lines - such as here for the Phil Collins Indoor tour »Into the Light«.

In der nächsten Entwurfsphase werden die Skizzen zur beweglichen, computergenerierten Perspektive, die die präzise Umsetzung in eine montable Konstruktion zuläßt: hier Kuppel und Schirm der Bühne.

In the next stage of design, the sketches become a movable, computer-generated perspective which can be precisely converted into a construction which can be actually be built. Here, the cupola and shield over the stage.

Die bewegliche Bühnenoberkonstruktion ist dank ihrer mobilen Flügel in der Lage, sehr unterschiedliche Räume zu formulieren.

The moveable stage super-structure can be used to create very different spaces, thanks to its mobile wings.

Barock: Bridges to Babylon, Rolling Stones

Baroque: Bridges to Babylon, Rolling Stones

Mark Fisher, 1997/98

Die bisher letzte Rolling Stones Tour »Bridges to Babylon« sollte eher »opulent als dekadent sein« (Fisher). Die Inspirationsquelle des Architekten war hier die Barockarchitektur von Europa bis Mexiko – insbesondere die stolzen katholischen Kirchenbauten. Die über 50 Meter breite und 24 Meter hohe Bühne wird von der elliptischen Mega-Videoleinwand majorisiert: ein riesiger Fernseher für 60.000 bis 100.000 Zuschauer gleichzeitig. Je nach Song und Inszenierung wird das Bühnenmonstrum zum rotkitschigen red-light district, zur

The last Rolling Stones' tour up to now, »Bridges to Babylon«, was intended to be more »opulent than decadent« (Fisher). The source of inspiration for the architect was baroque architecture from Europe to Mexico - especially proud Catholic churches. The stage, which is over 50 metres wide and 24 metres high, is dominated by an elliptical mega video screen, a huge television for 60,000 to 100,000 people to watch at the same time. Depending on the song and the stage setting, the stage monster turns into a kitsch red-light district

blaugrünen Musikbox oder zur grellen Laserkanone; dies technisch zu jeder Zeit und bei jedem Wetter mit immer gleichem Ergebnis zu erreichen, ist wahrscheinlich die größte Leistung dieser Show. Ganz passend zum Titel »Bridges to Babylon« ist ein Stahlsteg, der im Laufe des Konzerts über die Zuschauer hinweg zu einer zweiten Kleinstbühne geklappt wird. Dieser Steg ist nur für knapp eine Minute zu sehen und kostet etwa eine Million Dollar. Ein Beitrag zum Thema »Star und Bad in der Menge«. Und vielleicht auch das Signal zum Ende eines Trends. Mark Fisher und auch die Rolling Stones glauben nicht mehr an die Zukunft von Stadionkonzerten – so könnte die Mega-Stage Architecture bald schon Vergangenheit sein.

or a blue-green juke box or a garish laser cannon. Technically, this can be done at any time and in any weather and always with the same results. This is probably the most outstanding achievement of this show. In accordance with the title »Bridges to Babylon«, there is a steel bridge which extends over the heads of the audience during the show until it reaches another very small stage. This bridge can only be seen for just over a minute and cost around one million dollars, merely to enable the image of »star plus walkabout«. And perhaps also a sign of the end of a trend. Mark Fisher and the Rolling Stones as well no longer believe in the future of stadium concerts. Megastage architecture could soon be a thing of the past.

Der Titel der Show wird durch einen ausschiebbaren Brückensteg umgesetzt, der von der Hauptbühne zur »Club«-Bühne führt (vgl. auch S. 118/119).

The title of the show is represented by a retractable bridge, going from the main stage to the »club« stage (cf. pp. 118/119).

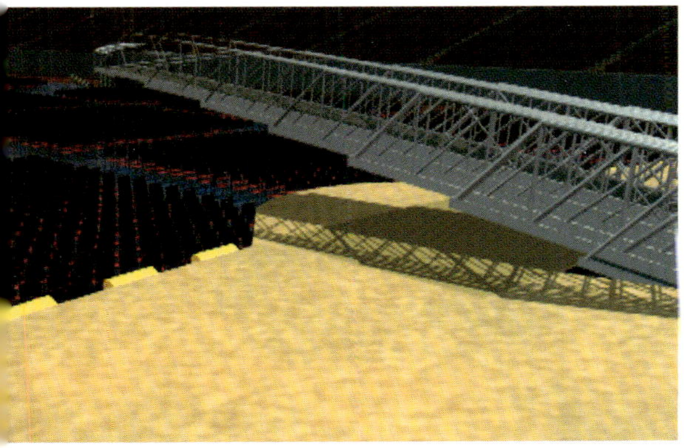

Es gehört inzwischen zur Tradition bei Mark Fisher, für die Stones figürlich zu arbeiten – bei »Bridges to Babylon« sind diese ausgesprochen üppig ausgefallen. Auch hier werden alle Entwürfe computergeneriert erstellt.

With Mark Fisher, it is now traditional to work for the Stones with figures – in »Bridges to Babylon«, these are especially opulent. All the drafts were also generated by computers.

Links: Ausschnitt aus dem Live-Konzert – die Brücke ist weniger als eine Minute lang zu sehen.
Rechts: Hauptbühne vor dem Beginn der Show.
Nächste Seiten: Die Hauptbühne in voller Aktion.

Left: During the concert – The bridge can only be seen for less than a minute.
Right: Main stage before the beginning of the show.
Following pages: The main stage in full action.

4. Akt
Act 4

Event-Architektur
Event architecture

Tourenmeister: Gästepavillon Mercedes-Benz

Eine Klasse für sich: A-Motion Tour

Touring master: Mercedes-Benz guest pavilion

A class of its own: the A-Motion Tour

Autos sind mobil. Formel-1-Boliden beispielsweise können, wenn auch nicht auf den eigenen vier Rädern, in Containern durch die ganze Welt transportiert werden. Dann fahren sie los, so schnell wie möglich. Bauten, die Autos begleiten, müssen es mit ihrer Schnelligkeit aufnehmen können, zumindest symbolisch. Im Zuge der Markteinführung eines völlig neu konzipierten Kompakt-Autos hat der Hersteller nicht gewartet, bis die potentiellen Käufer zu ihm in die Showrooms kommen, sondern er fliegt zu ihnen. »Zu den Leuten, in die Herzen der Städte, und zwar europaweit, gehen!« heißt seine Devise. | Das Thema lautet hier: Fliegende Bauten im Dienste der Kommunikation und Verkaufsförderung. Kommerzielle Bauten eben. Und gemeint ist hier nicht der mobile Messepavillon, sondern eben die Bühne für eine Idee, eine Vision, die dann zum Produkt werden darf. Kein Wunder, wenn die Automobilindustrie sich auf dieses Terrain am weitesten vorwagt. Fliegende Bauten und schnelle Autos sind ein tolles Paar. Die Präsentation eines neuen Autos, die Präsenz eines Unternehmens auf dem Nürburgring oder die Promotion durch einen Event – sie alle sind im Grunde Werbeaktionen der neuen Generation. In einer Einladung zum Haltepunkt des fliegenden Bauwerks am Berliner Alexanderplatz steht: »Unsere Tour ist kein Theater, kein Konzert, keine Autoausstellung!« Nein, es ist alles zusammen. Nacheinander, miteinander, gekonnt durcheinander. | Trotzdem, oder gerade deswegen, ist es weiterhin eine Aufgabe für den Architekten. Andreas Theilig hat beispielsweise für die wohl bekannteste Promotion Tournee der letzten Jahre, die A-Motion Tour, mit der Kraft des Kubus kokettiert. | Für einen Gästepavillon der Mercedes-Benz AG hat man eine fächerförmige Grundstruktur festgelegt. Kein Zu-

Und gemeint ist nicht der mobile Messepavillon, sondern eben die Bühne für eine Idee, eine Vision, die dann zum Produkt werden darf.

Cars are mobile creatures. Formula 1 missiles, for example, can simply be transported all over the world in containers, if not on their own four wheels. They then drive off as fast as they can. The buildings which are used as a backdrop for cars must be able to cope with such speed, at least symbolically. In the course of launching a completely new compact-car design, the manufacturer does not wait until potential customers come into the showroom but flies directly to meet them. »To the people, to all the cities of Europe!» is his maxim. | Here, the subject is temporary buildings in the service of communication and the promotion of sales. In other words, commercial buildings. The mobile trade-fair pavilion is not meant here but the stage for an idea, a vision, which can then turn into a product. No wonder that the automobile industry has ventured furthest into this terrain. Temporary buildings and fast cars go well together. The

fall, sondern eine Referenz an die Hausform jenes Herzstückes des Konzerns, das Design Center heißt und in dem die Prototypen der Serienfahrzeuge erdacht, gebaut und getestet werden. | Und es ist eine interessante Ingenieursarbeit. Anders als bei den Megabühnen der Popstars, wo meist die Urkonstruktion aus bewährten Fachwerkstahlwerkträgern besteht, die einem Meccano-Baukasten verwandt sind, wird bei diesen kleineren und individuellen Bauaufgaben jeweils die Unterkonstruktion für die Standfestigkeit neu zu überdenken sein. Und wenn eine dieser Bühnen noch »Feuer speien« oder für komplizierte Tanzchoreographien tauglich sein soll, heißt es tief in die konstruktive Trickkiste zu greifen. Die beiden Bauwerke, die hier vorgestellt werden, sind Meisterwerke ihrer Zunft: nicht nur elegant und komplex, sondern auch stabil und flexibel.

presentation of a company's new car in the Nürburgring or promotion by means of an event – they are all basically advertising campaigns of the new generation. An invitation to visit the stop-over location of a temporary construction in the Alexanderplatz in Berlin reads: »Our tour is not theatre, nor is it a concert or a car exhibition!« No, it is all of these together. One after the other, one with the other and skilfully mixed with each other. | Nevertheless or precisely because of this, it is a task for the architect. For the probably best-known »tour« of recent years, the A-Motion Tour, for example, Andreas Theilig played around with the potential of the cube. | A basic fan-shaped structure was stipulated for the guest pavilion of Mercedes-Benz AG. No coincidence but a reference to the company's centrepiece, the Design Center in which the prototypes of mass-produced vehicles are envisioned, constructed and tested. | And it is an interesting piece of engineering work. In contrast to the mega-stages of the pop stars, where the basic construction is composed of steel beams like a »Meccano« building, the sub-construction for these smaller and individual construction jobs will have to be re-thought in terms of stability. And if one of these stages is to be suitable for »spouting fire« or for complicated choreography, it will be necessary to dig deep into the box of building tricks. The two structures presented here are masterworks of their kind not only elegant and complex but also stable and flexible.

The mobile trade-fair pavilion is not meant here but the stage for an idea, a vision, which can then turn into a product.

Tourenmeister: Gästepavillon Mercedes-Benz

Touring master: Mercedes-Benz guest pavilion

Greschbach, 1994 - 96

Veranstaltungen, Präsentationen, Bewirtungen – dies ist der Sinn und Zweck des fingerförmigen und reisefähigen Pavillons. Ein kleiner Bruder des großen Sindelfinger Design Center, das der Architekt Renzo Piano für die Abteilung des Mercedes-Chef-Designers Sacco entworfen hatte. Auch hier werden gebogene Dächer eingebaut, die so verlegt werden, daß sie seitliche Oberbelichtung zulassen. Die grundsätzliche Lage hier indes war komplizierter. Der Pavillon sollte mindestens bei acht Läufen der deutschen Tourenwagen-Meisterschaft präsentiert werden. In 36 Stunden Bauzeit sind die 1.250 Quadratmeter Grundfläche aufgebaut. Freitragende Bogendächer, Stahl-Rahmen-Konstruktion mit Rohrstützen, Aluminium-Sandwich-Elemente: So heißen die Zutaten, wenn ein fliegender Bau entsteht. Bei allen »wandernden« Konstruktionen muß immer besondere Aufmerksamkeit auf die Gründung gelegt werden. Höhenverstellbare Auflager der Rohrstützen sorgen dafür, daß Unebenheiten und unterschiedliche Niveaus ausgeglichen werden können.

Events, presentations and catering are the intrinsic functions of the finger-shaped travelling pavilion. It is the little brother of the large Design Center in Sindelfingen which architect Renzo Piano designed for the department of Mercedes' chief designer, Sacco. Curved roofs are also used for the guest pavilion. They are mounted so that they allow light to enter from the side through skylights. But the basic situation was more complicated. The idea was to present the pavilion during eight rounds of the German saloon-car championships. 36 hours are needed to erect it on an area of 1,250 square metres. Self-supporting curved roofs, aluminium sandwich elements and a steel frame construction with pipe supports were the ingredients when this temporary building was created. For all »travelling« constructions, special attention must always be paid to the footing. Height-adjustable pads for the pipe supports ensure that any variation of levels can be evened out.

Der relativ große Baukörper (circa 1.250 Quadratmeter) wirkt in Dachauf- und Seitenansicht beinahe kleinteilig. Dafür sorgen fünf gebogene Dachschalen, die sich so überlappen, daß seitliche Oberlichter eingebaut werden können.

The relatively large construction (approx. 1,250 square metres) looks almost small-sectioned when seen from the side or the air. This is due to the curved roof shells which overlap each other so that skylights can be built in at the sides.

Der außen stark gegliederte Baukörper läßt dank einer leichten Konstruktion im Inneren großen, flexibel nutzbaren Raum für unterschiedliche Veranstaltungen zu.

The large and flexible interior space of the construction, which is broken down into many components on the outside, can be used for many different types of event.

Eine Klasse für sich: A-Motion Tour

A class of its own: the A-Motion Tour

Kauffmann Theilig & Partner, 1997

In einfachen Konzepten liegt die Kraft. Andreas Theilig besinnt sich auf den geometrischen Urtyp Kubus – als Idee, als Zeichen, Bild oder stadträumliches Element. Der Kubus wird auf diese Weise zum Orientierungsort in der Stadt: seine architektonische Kraft wirkt wie ein Magnet, und dann wird dieser Kubus auch noch zur Bühne. Für den Autotyp, den es bekannt zu machen gilt: die neue A-Klasse von Mercedes-Benz. Ein weißes Zelt wird aufgespannt, benutzt den Kubus als Ganzes, das sanft und textil aufgeteilt wird. Geometrische Stringenz in Harmonie mit den wogenden Zeltplanen. 18 Meter Kantenlänge, 1.100 Quadratmeter Bühne überragt von 48 plastisch geformten Holzstäben, die den Kubus markieren, verbunden durch 27 Stahlknoten, diagonal stabilisiert durch Stahlseile. Auf der Plattform stehen mobile Boxen, Café-Gestühl und als Hauptdarsteller natürlich die A-Klasse. Die Plattform wird abends als Bühne der Theater-Avantgarde-Gruppe La Fura dels Baus überlassen.

Power through simplicity. Andreas Theilig reflects on the basic geometrical shape of the cube – as an idea, a sign, an image or an element of the city. The cube thus becomes a landmark within the city. Its architectonic power acts like a magnet and then it becomes a stage for the new A-Class saloon car from Mercedes-Benz, the new automobile to be introduced. A white tent is erected which uses the cube as a whole, dividing it up gently with fabric – geometric astringency in harmony with the curved lines of the tent. The edges are 18 metres long and there are 1,100 square metres of stage, towered over by 48 sculptured wooden rods which are connected by 27 steel nodes and stabilised diagonally by steel cables. Mobile boxes rest on the stage as café seating and, of course, the A-Class as the protagonist. In the evening the platform is used as a stage for the avant-garde theatre group, La Fura dels Baus.

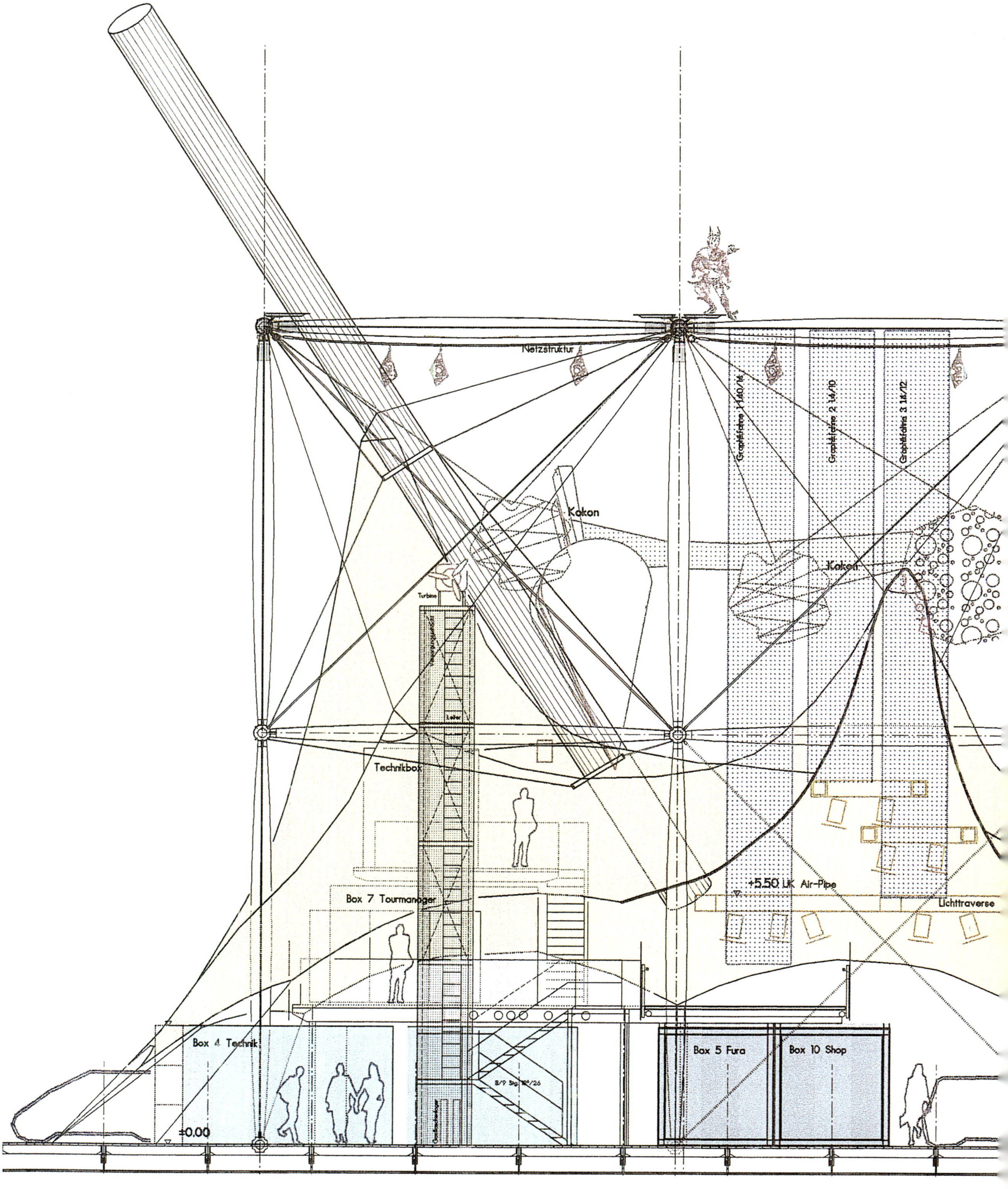
Netzstruktur
Kokon
Kokon
Turbine
Technikbox
Box 7 Tourmanager
+5.50 UK Air-Pipe
Lichttraverse
Box 4 Technik
±0.00
Box 5 Fura
Box 10 Shop

Architekten:

Kauffmann Theilig & Partner

Kommunikationskonzept:

Atelier Markgraph

Bau: Ambrosius Messebau

Eventkonzeption und -koordination:

Clausecker & Bingel

Architects:

Kauffmann Theilig & Partner

Communications concept:

Atelier Markgraph

Construction:

Ambrosius Messebau

Event conception and coordination:

Clausecker & Bingel

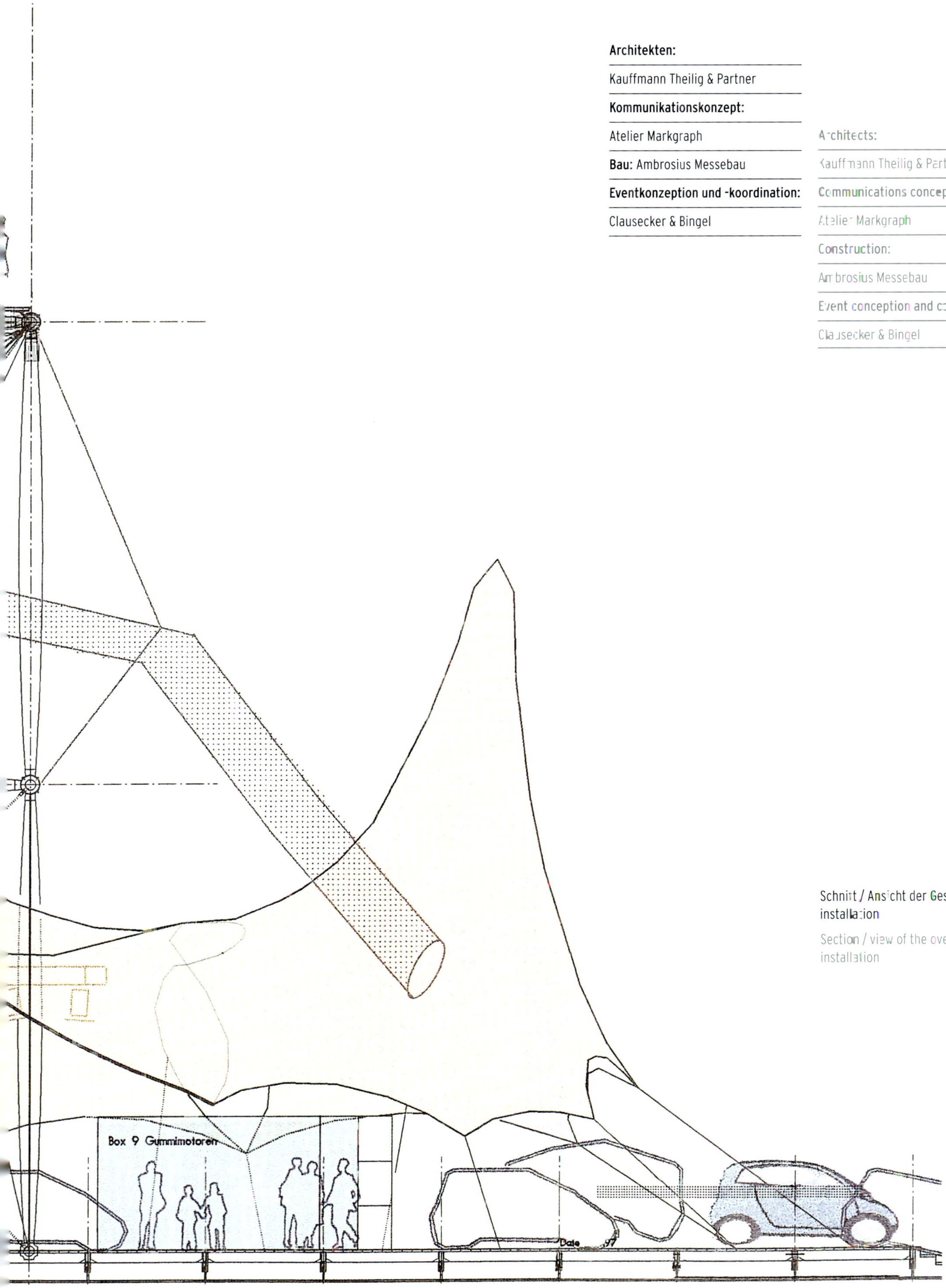

Schnitt / Ansicht der Gesamt-installation

Section / view of the overall installation

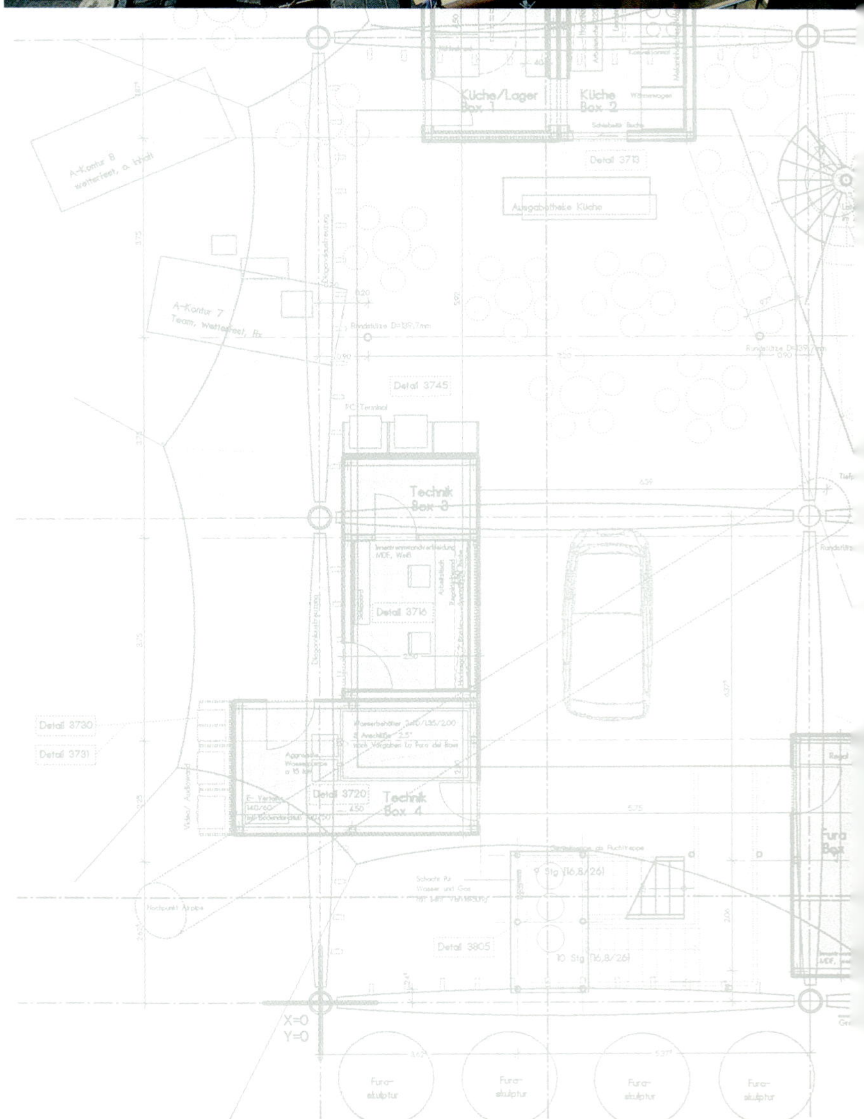

Oben: Bei einer Aufbauzeit von nur drei Tagen mußte die Fundamentskonstruktion entsprechend mobil gehalten werden. Sie besteht aus Betonfertigteilen mit eingehängten, höhenverstellbaren Füßen.
Mitte: Der Kubus besteht aus 48 Holzstäben, die durch Stahlgußknoten verbunden werden.

Top: Given a construction time of only three days, the foundations had to be kept mobile. They consist of prefabricated concrete sections with height-adjustable feet.
Middle: The cube consists of 48 wooden rods connected by cast-steel nodes.

Oben: Normaler Alltag beim Aufbau fliegender Bauten; fast wie auf einer richtigen Baustelle, nur geschieht hier alles im dreifachen Tempo.
Unten: Für die Aufführung der Künstler von La Fura wurde oben in den Kubus ein Netz eingezogen.

Top: Normal everyday occurrence in the construction of temporary buildings, almost like a real building site but three times as fast.
Below: A net was incorporated in the cube for the performance of the La Fura artistes.

Menschen und fliegende Bauten - die Unterschiede scheinen minimal, ob es sich nun um die Arbeiter handelt, die die Bühne bauen oder die Künstler, die die Bühne nutzen. In beiden Fällen ist es eine perfekte Performance.

People and temporary buildings - the differences appear to be minimal, whether the people are those who build the stage or the artistes who use it. In both cases, the performance is perfect.

Seiten 142-145: Kubus und Zelt im Prozeß: 1. Vor der Präsentation: geheimnisvoll verpackt. 2. Am Höhepunkt der Vorstellung von La Fura: feuersprühend und phantasievoll.

Pages 142 to 145: Cube and tent in process. 1. Mysteriously packaged before the presentation 2. The climax of La Fura's performance, with fire and fantasy.

Heute im Kub

mobil
Gummimobil Wettbewerb
Gummimobil Wettbewerb

reaktion
simbiosis
eVent
verÄnderung

La Fura dels Baus entwickelte das Stück »Simbiosis« speziell für das gemeinsame Projekt mit Daimler-Benz. Es handelt von Transformation, Evolution, Regeneration – Übergang, Wandel, Entwicklung und Erneuerung.

La Fura dels Baus developed the piece, »Simbiosis«, specially for the joint project with Daimler-Benz. It deals with transformation, evolution and regeneration.

»Der Kubus als Idee: Er ist stadträumliche Markierung, erinnerbares Zeichen, Bühne, intelligente temporäre Konstruktion!«
Andreas Theilig

»The cube as an idea. It is a landmark within the city, a memorable sign, a stage and an intelligent temporary construction!«
Andreas Theilig

PICK
MÖVENPICK

Die A-Motion in den Städten Berlin, Stuttgart, Hamburg, Neapel, und Madrid (von links nach rechts).

The A- Motion in Berlin, Stuttgart, Hamburg, Naples and Madrid (from left to right).

Vorherige Seiten: Großer Auftritt vor der Oper: Die A-Motion residiert zu Füßen der Frankfurter Hochhaus-Skyline.

Previous pages: Large-scale performance in front of the opera house: the A-Motion at the feet of the Frankfurt skyscraper skyline.

By the way ... 180 Leute reisen 185 Tage 11.000 Kilometer zu 21 Städten Europas; 54 Trucks bewegen 2 Sets des Kubus, 2 Generatorenausrüstungen; 4 Busse, 20 Kleinbusse, 10 PKWs, 4 Wohnmobile, 2 Toilettenzüge; 644.258 Besucher.

By the way ... 180 people spend 185 days travelling 11,000 kilometres to 21 cities in Europe; 54 trucks move 2 cube sets, 2 sets of generator equipment; There are 4 busses, 20 minibuses, 10 cars, 2 caravans, 2 toilet convoys and 644,258 visitors.

5. Akt
Act 5

Mobilität auf der Bühne
Mobility on stage

Im finalen Akt – und das ist in diesem Buch durchaus programmatisch zu verstehen – liegt die Betonung auf dem zweiten Titelbegriff: der Bühne. Und trotzdem dient dieser Abschnitt nicht ausschließlich dem Thema Bühnenkulissen und Bühnenarchitektur. Stattdessen wählen wir einen Ausschnitt, einen Fokus aus, der zu unserem Thema paßt; dort, wo in Anlehnung an Schinkels Vorgänger das Architektonisch-Räumliche so weit ausgeprägt ist, daß man von Bauwerken sprechen kann. Oder auch von »Theaterorten« oder »Theaterräumen«, wie einer der Hauptprotagonisten dieses Kapitels, der Architekt und Raumkünstler Hans Dieter Schaal, schreibt. | Schaals mobile Bühnen sind der eine Pol, um den es in diesem Akt geht: Saubere geometrische Gebilde, fast bis zum Abstraktum reduziert. Hans Dieter Schaal beschränkt sich auf die drei klassischen Dimensionen des architektonischen Raumes. Baut in geometrischer Strenge sozusagen die jeweilige Arche, die die »Handlung wie ein Schneckenhaus umfaßt«. Die Einhausungen des Herrn Schaal sind beides: optimale Hintergründe und Vordergründe sowie eine gleichzeitige Verbeugung vor der Arbeit des Raumkünstlers, der vielleicht die wahre Seele des Baukünstlers und Baumeisters ist. | Eine Antipode solcher puristischen Arrangements, sozusagen die große Oper im Vergleich zum Kammertheater, ist, wie Peter Metzler über »Porgy und Bess« auf der Freilichtbühne Bregenz schrieb: »ein Feuersturm, der die monumentale Seebühne und mit ihr die rund 7.000 Zuschauer fassende Arena in ein mystisches Licht taucht«. Wenn sich Schaal auf die Ruhe der Nach-Nach-Moderne besinnt, dann erinnert Bregenz noch ein bißchen an Maschinenästhetik, und die Macht der Dynamik verweist

Mit den Aufbauten auf der flexiblen Seebühne wird eine weitere Dimension des Bauens eingeführt; es ist die Welt der Düfte, der Wärme und der Kälte aus der Natur.

In the final act – and this is to be understood as part of the book's programme – the emphasis is placed on the other word in the title, the stage itself. Nevertheless, this section is not exclusively devoted to the topic of stage backgrounds and stage architecture. Instead, we pick out an extract, a focus, which fits in with our topic; the point where, following Schinkel's predecessors, the architectural-cum-spatial is revealed to such an extent that it is possible to speak of buildings. Or also of »theatrical locations» or »theatrical spaces«, as one of the main protagonists of this chapter, the architect and artist of space, Hans Dieter Schaal, writes. | Schaal's mobile stages are a magnetic pole at the centre of this act: clear and geometrical structures, almost reduced to an abstraction. Dieter Schaal restricts himself to three classic dimensions of architectural space, building an arch with geometric strictness, so to say, which »accommodates the action like a snail's shell«. The housings of Mr. Schaal are both optimum backgrounds and foregrounds as well as a simultaneous bow to the work of the artist of space – perhaps the real soul of the architect and master builder. | As an antipode to such purist arrangements, so to say grand opera in comparison to studio theatre, there is that which Peter Metzler, for example, wrote about »Porgy and Bess« on the open-

auf die Zeiten der klassischen Moderne. | Und wenn dort in Bregenz zum Beispiel ein Stück Highway aus Beton und Holz als Kulisse aufgerichtet wird, dann werden damit locker die baulichen Ausmaße eines Nationenpavillons auf einer Expo erreicht. Es wird schlagartig klar, daß Statik, Standfestigkeit und Brandschutz hier einen Problemhorizont erreichen können, der den Bau eines festen Einfamilienhauses nahezu als lächerliche Kleinigkeit erscheinen läßt. | Mit den Aufbauten auf der flexiblen Seebühne wird zusätzlich eine weitere Dimension des Bauens eingeführt; es ist die Welt der Düfte, der Wärme und Kälte aus der Natur. Damit ist nicht etwa nur der künstliche Feuersturm über Catfish Row gemeint, der gekonnt pyromanisch und illusionistisch über die Bühne fegt, sondern die Symbiose aus Seebühne und Bodenseelandschaft, die sich jeden Abend neu ergibt: So manches Seegewitter kam zur Aufführungszeit und gab der festgelegten Bühnenhandlung einen unerwarteten Rahmen … .

The structures erected on the flexible floating stage introduced a further dimension to the art of building: the smells, the warmth and the coldness of nature.

air stage in Bregenz: »A firestorm which engulfs the monumental lake-enclosed stage in a mystical light and, with it, the arena containing an audience of around 7,000 people«. Whereas Schaal reflects on the peace of the post-post modern, Bregenz reminds us a little of the machine aesthetic, and the power of dynamics refers us to the times of classical modernity. | And when in Bregenz a piece of highway made of concrete and wood is erected as a background, for example, the dimensions of a national pavilion at an Expo are easily reached. It abruptly becomes clear that statics, stability and fire protection can here reach their problematic limits, making the building of a single-family house an almost laughable trifle. | The structures erected on the flexible floating stage introduced a further dimension to the art of building: the smells, the warmth and the coldness of nature. This does not just refer to the artificial fire tower over Catfish Row which passes over the stage in a skilled pyromaniacal and illusionistic sweep but also the symbiosis of stage-on-lake and the landscape of Lake Constance which renews itself every evening. Many a storm took place during the performance and encompassed the action on stage within an unexpected framework … .

Antikes Fragment: Die Intendanten

Antique fragment: Die Intendanten

Hans Dieter Schaal, Bundeskunsthalle Bonn, 1997

Die Uraufführung eines Theaterstücks an einem Ort, der nicht Theater, sondern Museum ist. Folge: Die Bühne muß improvisiert werden. Dies ist heutzutage keine Ausnahme, wenn es wie hier um eine experimentelle Oper geht. Der Inhalt ist einfach und trotzdem bedeutungsschwer: Er handelt von einer komprimierten Theatergeschichte zwischen der Antike und heute. Schaal: »Aufgebaut wurde eine angedeutete archäologische Situation mit Ruinenfragmenten«. Hans Dieter Schaal transportiert mit seiner Kulisse klassische Motive aus der Bauwelt – Scheibe, Treppe, Fenster, Dreieck, Quadrat. Natürlich alle als tiefgründige Bedeutungsträger. Denn die Scheibe zum Beispiel bildet die große Erdenscheibe ab, die eigentlich Kugel ist. Der übrige Rest des Arrangements mit Leiter und Stuhl geht als doppelter Hochsitz durch. Wer beobachtet wen? Die Schauspieler die Zuschauer oder umgekehrt? Die Schauspieler die Schauspieler? Schaal gibt eine schlüssige Eigeninterpretation ab: »Die Geschichte ist wie eine Rätselstunde.«

The first performance of a play at a location which is not a theatre but a museum. The consequence is that the stage had to be improvised. Nowadays, this is no exception when an experimental opera is involved as in this case. The content is simple, yet heavy with meaning. It is a compressed history of the theatre between the ancient world and today. As Schaal comments, »An implied architectural situation was constructed with fragments of ruins«. With this backdrop, Hans Dieter Schaal transports classical motifs from the world of architecture – the disc, stairs, window, triangle and square, all of which, of course, being bearers of profound meaning. The disc, for example, represents the earth as disc although it is actually a ball. The rest of the arrangements with ladder and stool is meant as a double high-seat. Who is watching whom? The actors watching the audience or vice versa, or the actors watching the actors? Schaal himself presents his own conclusive interpretation: »The story is a round of puzzles.«

»Die Inszenierung schwebt zwischen Archäologie und Utopie«, sagt Hans Dieter Schaal. Fragmente und Büsten von Beteiligten der Theatergeschichte sollen dieses Statement mit Leben erfüllen.

»The production hovers between archaeology and utopia«, says Hans Dieter Schaal. Fragments and busts of participants from the history of the theatre are intended to fill this statement with life.

Die Welt als runde schiefe Ebene - zweifellos der Mittelpunkt dieser Installation für »Die Intendanten« von Franz Hummel in der Regie von Dominik Neuner.

The world as a slanted, circular plane - without doubt the centrepoint of this installation for »Die Intendanten«, a play by Franz Hummel, directed by Dominik Neuner.

Die Architektur wächst mit: Die Zauberflöte

Self-transforming architecture: the Magic Flute

Hans Dieter Schaal, Wiesbaden, 1996

Ein Haus ist ein Haus. Genauer betrachtet ist es hier ein Vogelhaus, und das gehört zur Zauberflöte von Wolfgang Amadeus Mozart. So schreibt Schaal: »Großes Verwandlungstheater mit dem Vogelhausmotiv: Ganz winzig als Uhr, als echtes Vogelhaus, als Rucksack, Kinderhaus, Wohnhaus und Tempel.« Die Zauberflöte ist ein Stück, das sich mit dem Erwachsenwerden beschäftige. Sie stecke, sagt Schaal, voller Initiationsriten. »Die Architektur spielt mit. Sie verwandelt sich mit, dreht sich mit, schaukelt, tanzt und trauert.« Hier werden, analog zum richtigen Leben, Geschichten erzählt von Häusern, Treibhäusern, Vogelhäusern und Hochzeitshäusern. Streng genommen ist das Haus immer gleich. Schaal hat es wie einen Rahmen inszeniert. Mobil ist der Inhalt.

A house is a house. Here, to be more precise, a bird house, an integral part of the Magic Flute by Wolfgang Amadeus Mozart. As Schaal explains, »Large-scale theatre of transformation with the bird-house motif: small as a clock, as a real bird house, as a rucksack, as a children's house, as a residential building and as a temple.« The Magic Flute deals with the problems of growing up. It is full of rites of initiation, says Schaal. »The architecture also plays a role. It changes as the action changes, turns when the others turn and swings, dances and grieves.« Similar to real life, stories are told of houses, greenhouses, bird houses and marriage houses. Strictly speaking, the house is always the same but Schaal has designed it as a framework. It is the content which is mobile.

Die Zauberflöte ist eine Oper, die vom Erwachsenwerden handelt – da müssen auch die Häuser mitwachsen.

The Magic Flute is an opera which deals with the theme of growing up. The houses therefore have to grow as well.

Vorherige Seiten: Das Vogelhaus als Bühnenrahmen und -accessoire in vielen Größen.

Previous pages: The bird house as a stage framework and scenery accessory in many sizes.

Der Prototyp eines Vogelhäuschens eignet sich auch als Heimstatt für Menschen - zumindest auf der Bühne. Regie dieser Aufführung von Mozarts Zauberflöte: Dominik Neuner.

The prototype of a bird house is also suitable as a home for people - at least on the stage. This production of Mozart's Magic Flute was directed by Dominik Neuner.

Schmelztiegel der Gefühle: Rigoletto

A Melting Pot of Emotions: Rigoletto

Hans Dieter Schaal, Münster, 1995

Eine trapezförmige Box, deren Frontseite geöffnet wird, ist der Spielort, wo auf dieser Bühne Öffentliches mit Privatem verschmilzt und das Wohnzimmer zur Straße wird. Ein Gebilde für »tragische Emotionen« (Hans Dieter Schaal). Die Akteure agieren in einem Szenario, das keinen eigenen Ort besitzt und zugleich überall stattfinden kann. Durch diesen hohen und engen Raum, wird der Eindruck erzeugt, die Darsteller befänden sich in einem tiefen Schacht. Lichteffekte steigern diese Wirkung, verschärfen Kontraste. Für die Schauspieler, für die Zuschauer: Die Nerven liegen bloß … .

A trapezium-shaped box, open at the front, is the setting in which the public and the private are fused together and the living room becomes the street outside, forming a background for »tragic emotions« (Hans Dieter Schaal). The actors perform in a scenario which itself has no location but which, at the same time, can be anywhere. The high and narrow enclosed space of the box creates the impression that the performers are in a deep shaft. Light effects increase this feeling and emphasize the contrasts, exposing the nerves of both actors and audience … .

Diese Seiten: Die Box wird zum Schmelztiegel der Gefühle, und die Akteure sitzen gefangen im Schattenspiel von Hell und Dunkel.

These pages: The box becomes a melting pot of emotions and the performers are imprisoned in the interplay of light and dark.

Nächste Seiten: Totale. Das heillose Durcheinander der Stühle weist auf überkochende Emotionen in einem engen Raum hin, der keine Flucht zuläßt. Die Fenster im Hintergrund scheinen den Weg in eine andere Welt zu deuten, die sich von dieser dunklen Realität abhebt. Regie: Dominik Neuner

Following pages: The total confusion of the stools represents overheated emotions in the narrow space from which there is no escaping. The windows in the background seem to point the way to another world which is apart from this dark reality. Director: Dominik Neuner

Mobile Bühne: Boulevard Solitude

Mobile stage: Boulevard Solitude

Hans Dieter Schaal, Frankfurt, 1998

In dieser Inszenierung des Boulevard Solitude von Hans Werner Henze nimmt Hans Dieter Schaal das Thema wörtlich: Die Drehbühne ist in sich mobil und hat durch ihre Bewegung innerhalb weniger Sekunden jeweils eine sehr unterschiedliche Präsenz. Mobilität während ein und derselben Aufführung. Auch dies ist eine Definition von mobiler Bühne. In dieser Inszenierung kommt hinzu, daß die übliche Architekturszenerie einer kleinen Stadt zu sehen ist. Motive, aus denen Stadt besteht: Kurven, Rechtecke, Treppen, die je nach Perspektive zum Vorder- oder Hintergrund werden. »Alle meine Bühnenbilder sind mobil«, sagt Schaal, »sie werden jeden Abend auf- und abgebaut, aber der Bau einer Drehbühne ist die Steigerung!«

In this production of Boulevard Solitude by Hans Werner Henze, Hans Dieter Schaal takes a literal approach to the theme. The rotating stage is itself mobile and, within just a few seconds, takes on a completely different aura as a result of its motion. Mobility during one and the same performance. This is also a definition of the mobile stage. Another factor is that, in this production, the usual architectural scenery of a small town can be seen, with motifs that themselves create the town such as curves, rectangles and steps which turn into the foreground or background depending on the perspective. »All my stage sets are mobile«, says Schaal, »They are constructed and dismantled every evening but the construction of a rotating stage goes one step further!«

Rasch wechselnde Eindrücke, vielfältig wie in einer richtigen Stadt, auf nur einer Bühne und in wenigen Stunden. Möglich gemacht durch eine Drehbühne (vgl. S. 175).

Rapidly changing impressions, multi-faceted like a real city, but only on a stage and within a few hours. Made possible by a rotating stage (cf. p. 175).

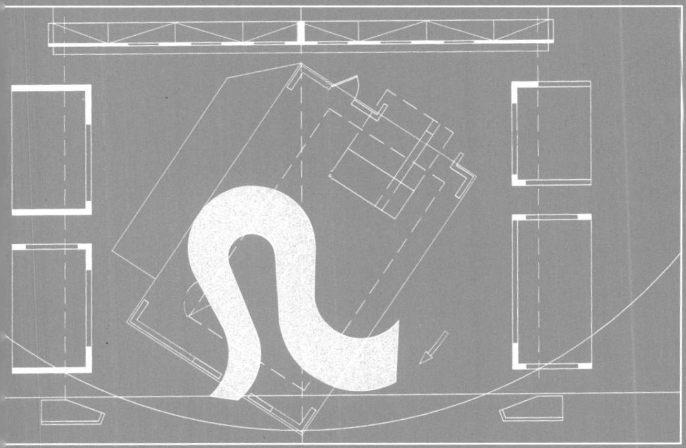

Die Zeichnungen verdeutlichen, wie durch die Drehung des zentralen Baukörpers mit der Treppe immer wieder neue veränderte Ansichten entstehen.

The drawings illustrate how new viewpoints are repeatedly created with the staircase by rotation of the central element.

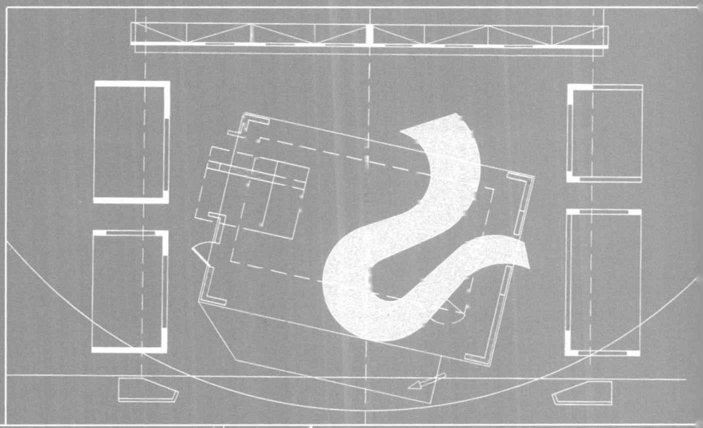

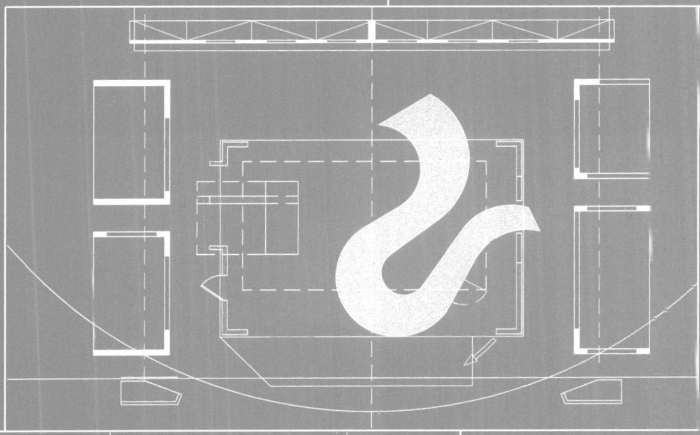

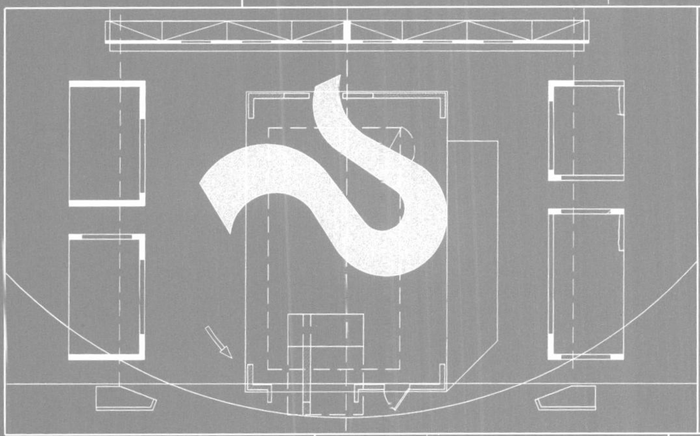

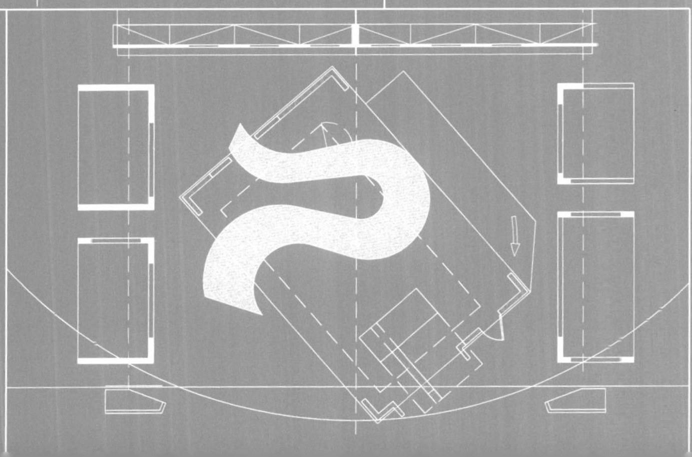

Oben und rechts: Auch diese Aufbauten weisen auf die geistige Provenienz Hans Dieter Schaals hin: die dreidimensionale räumliche Vorstellungskraft eines Architekten.

Above and right: These structural elements also point to the intellectual provenance of Hans Dieter Schaal, the three-dimensional imagination of an architect.

Nächste Seiten: Bilder aus einer kleinen Stadt. Mit wenigen Wänden, Öffnungen und Treppen immer wieder Räume in Bewegung setzen. Regie: Nicolas Brieger

Following Pages: Pictures from a small town. With just a few walls, openings and staircases, spaces are kept in continuous movement. Director: Nicolas Brieger

Klipp, klapp: Nabucco

Bend and fold: Nabucco

Stefanos Lazaridis, Bregenz, 1993/94

Nabucco von Giuseppe Verdi war 1994 die erste Produktion in Bregenz auf einer neuen Seebühne, die auf über 200 Holzpfählen verankert ist. Mit etwa 7.000 Zuschauern und 400 Akteuren ist die Bregenzer Bühne jetzt das größte Unternehmen dieser Art auf der Welt. Das Konzept für Nabucco ist in besonderer Weise mobil: Kulissen und Bühne lassen sich kippen oder hochstellen, damit die Bühne partiell auch einmal zur Kulisse werden kann. Das passiert hydraulisch, da ein schnelles und lautloses Wechseln der Schauplätze hier nicht mit Schnürböden und dergleichen bewerkstelligt werden kann. Die Inszenierung ist auf Fernwirkung angelegt, lebt besonders von der Höhe der Kulisse. Das Paradoxon einer Bühne besteht immer darin, daß sie eigentlich schwer und für die Ewigkeit gebaut wirken soll, aber auch den Kriterien einer schnellen Montabilität und Demon-

In 1994, Nabucco by Giuseppe Verdi was the first production in Bregenz on the new lake stage which rested over 200 wooden posts. With approximately 7,000 members of the audience and 400 actors, the stage in Bregenz is the largest undertaking of its kind in the world. The concept for Nabucco is also mobile in a special way. The scenery and stage can be lowered or raised so that the stage can also partially become part of the scenery. This is done hydraulically because, here, a fast and noiseless change of scene cannot be achieved with flies or similar methods. The stage setting is designed to have an effect at a distance and especially depends on the height of the scenery. The paradox of a stage is that it should always appear heavy, as if built for eternity, but must still be capable of being constructed and dismantled quickly.

tabilität entsprechen muß. Leicht und trotzdem stabil sind hierbei kaschierte Holzplatten, die auf einem Stahlfachwerk montiert werden müssen. Dahinter sind Umkleideräume, Staubereiche, Auftritts- und Fluchtwege verborgen. Sie gehören mit zum mobilen Bereich. Lediglich der Orchestergraben und die Solistenumkleiden werden im Betonkern der Bühne fixiert. Bregenz und seine Bühneninstallationen sind, architektonisch betrachtet, Teil eines großen Ganzen. Denn es ist noch nicht lange her, daß 1980 für Schlechtwettertage und Indoor-Veranstaltungen unmittelbar anschließend das Festspiel- und Kongreßhaus entstanden und 1997 für den Probenbetrieb erweitert worden ist (Architektur: Much Untertrifaller und Helmut Dietrich). Friedrich Achleitner, Grandseigneur der österreichischen Architekturkritiker, behauptete: »Das Phänomen der Vorarlberger Baukünstler oder der Vorarlberger Bauschule ist das Modell einer regionalen Architekturentwicklung, das es in dieser Form, Ausprägung, Charakteristik, Dichte und Dynamik kein zweites Mal gibt!« In etwa gilt es auch für die Seebühne und ihre Ausbauten.

Light and nevertheless stable are the concealed wooden panels which have to be mounted on a steel frame. Behind this, there are hidden dressing rooms, storage areas, entrances and exits, all of which are mobile. Only the orchestra pit and the soloists' dressing rooms are permanent fixtures in the concrete core of the stage. Bregenz and its stage installations are, from an architectural point of view, part of a whole. After all, it is not so long ago that the festival and congress hall was erected (1980) shortly after for use during bad weather and for indoor events and then expanded in 1997 for rehearsals (architecture: Much Untertrifaller and Helmut Dietrich). Friedrich Achleitner, Austria's grand seigneur of architectural critics, maintains that »the phenomenon of Vorarlberg architects or the Vorarlberg school of architecture is a model of regional development in architecture which is the only one of its type as regards character, characteristics, density and dynamics!« About the same can be said for the lake stage and the scenery it uses.

Oben: Gesamtanlage der Bregenzer Festspiele mit Seebühne, Versorgungssteg, Anleger und Tribüne (vor der Erweiterung 1997) während einer Nabucco-Aufführung.
Unten: Aufbau des Bühnenbildes zu Nabucco 1993/94.

Top: All of the festival facilities in Bregenz together with the stage on the lake, the bridge for supplies, moorings and stands during a performance of Nabucco (before the extension in 1997).
Below: Construction of the stage set for Nabucco, 1993/94.

א תרצח
א תנאף
א תגנב
א תענה
א תחמד

לא תחמד
כבד את

Seiten 184-186: Variationen des Hauptaufbaus: ohne und mit Balkon, der an einem hydraulischen Hubkran hängt (vgl. auch S. 180). Rechts: Zweite Bühnenvariante mit Naturkulisse »Donner und Blitz«.

Pages 184 to 186: Variations of the main structure, with and without the balcony which is suspended from a hydraulic hoisting crane (cf. p. 180).
Right: Second stage variation with a natural setting of »thunder and lightning«.

Feuerzauber: Porgy und Bess

Fire magic: Porgy and Bess

Hans Schavernoch, Bregenz, 1997/1998

Ein Aufbau der Superlative. Ein Stück karibischer Vorstadt auf dem See. Zwischen einer Autoskulptur links bis zum Portalkran rechts liegen 110 Meter, zwischen der Bauschuttinsel im Vordergrund und dem Bühnenhintergrund 80 Meter. Der Abbruch-Highway ist bis zu 28 Meter hoch und als zentrale Installation natürlich die entscheidende Metapher zum Bühnenstück: Eine Autobahn, sogar noch in ihrer abgehobenen Form als Hochstraße, ist Symbol für Weg und Erfolg, hier bricht er genau dort ab, wo die Action ist: »Dummerweise ist dieser Highway jetzt kaputt«, sagt der Bühnenbildner Hans Schavernoch, »diese Bühne ist ein skeptischer Blick darauf, was wir für unsere Lebensziele halten, oder für den richtigen Weg.« Mit einer herkömmlichen architektonischen Bauaufgabe hat dies nichts mehr zu tun; eher ist ein Stück Stadt zu entwickeln, eines, das darüberhinaus künstlich auf alt und

A superlative stage-setting, a section of Caribbean suburbs on a lake. There are 110 metres between the car sculpture on the left and the gantry crane on the right and 80 metres between the island of rubble in the foreground and the stage backdrop. The broken-off highway is up to 28 metres high and, as a central element, is naturally the dominant metaphor of the opera. A highway, even when raised off the ground, is a symbol for travelling and arrival but, here, it stops abruptly where the action is. »Here, the highway is broken«, says set-designer, Hans Schavernoch, »and the stage presents a sceptical attitude towards what we hold to be our life's goals or the correct way of achieving them.« This has nothing to do with a conventional architectural task; the aim is rather to develop a piece of a city which is artificially designed to be old

heruntergekommen getrimmt wird. Und trotzdem wird hier im klassischen Sinn gebaut; die Planungszeit dauert etwa ein Jahr und den komplizierten Bauvorschriften ist selbstverständlich Folge zu leisten. Und damit dieser Bau nicht zum Fliegenden wird, gibt es eine Staffel von Vorschriften, wie auch ein Alarmszenario: ab einer Windgeschwindigkeit von 30 km/h wird sukzessive geräumt. Allerdings soll die Bühne Stürmen bis 120 km/h trotzen, ohne Schaden zu nehmen.

and dilapidated. The construction nevertheless employs classical methods. The planning period was around one year and the complicated building regulations had to be complied with. To ensure the stability of the structure, there were also a whole series of rules to be followed as well as emergency procedures. Above a wind speed of 30 kph, an evacuation has to be carried out. The stage, however, must still be able to withstand storm winds of up to 120 kph without being damaged.

SOMEBODY UP THERE LIKES

Diese Seite: Aufbaudetails
zur Highway-Konstruktion
von »Porgy und Bess«.
Seiten 190/ 191 und 194/195:
Stadt auf See - »Porgy und Bess«
während einer Aufführung 1997.

This page: Details of the superstructure for the highway construction of »Porgy and Bess«
Pages 190/191 and 194/195:
A city on a lake - »Porgy and Bess«
during a performance in 1997.

Einige Daten:

Eine computergesteuerte Licht- und Akustikanlage ermöglicht es, daß ein Sänger, der sich in einer Distanz zwischen 30 und 120 Meter zum Zuschauer, auf einer Bühnenbreite von 70 Metern und einem Höhenunterschied von 25 Metern bewegt, von jedem Zuschauer dort gehört wird, wo er ihn auch sieht. Alle, einschließlich Chor, singen mit Funkmikrofonen. Leistung der Akustikanlage: 70.000 Watt. Die Beleuchtung wird in 240 computergesteuerte Lichtkreise aufgeteilt, bestückt mit Halogenscheinwerfern. Zusätzlich können Scheinwerfer hinsichtlich Farbe, Richtung, Größe und Form gezielt eingesetzt werden, so daß sie alle Stimmungen zwischen Gewitter und Kerzenschein wiedergeben können

Some data:

A computer-controlled lighting and sound system which makes it possible for any member of the audience, irrespective of where they are sitting, to hear a singer who is between 30 and 120 metres away and moving about on a 70-metre-wide stage at a height of up to 25 metres. Everyone, including the choir, use radio microphones. Output of the sound system: 70, 000 watts. The lighting is composed of 240 computer-controlled light circuits, fitted with halogen spotlights. Spotlights can also be used in various colours, directions, sizes and shapes so that every mood from storm to candlelight can be simulated.

SOMEBODY UP THERE LIKES YOU.

Bildnachweise und Copyrights

Picture References and Copyrights

S. 12, 13	New Millennium Experience Co / QA Photos
S. 16, 17	Klaus Frahm / Contur GmbH
S. 20, 21	Bitter+Bredt
S. 24, 25	A. T. Schäfer
S. 28	New Millennium Experience Co / QA Photos
S. 31 - 33	Circus Krone
S. 35 - 37	Circus Roncalli
S. 38, 40	Annette Hauschild / Ostkreuz
S. 41	links: Annette Hauschild / Ostkreuz
	rechts: Jens Rötzsch / Ostkreuz
S. 42, 43	Plan: New Millennium Experience Co
S. 44, 45	Plan: New Millennium Experience Co
	oben / rechts: New Millennium Experience Co / QA Photos
S. 46 - 49	New Millennium Experience Co / QA Photos
S. 50	Shinkenchiku-Sha / Mitsuo Matsuoka
S. 55, 57, 58	Studio Mario Botta
S. 56, 59	Alo Zanetta
S. 60	Shinkenchiku-Sha / Mitsuo Matsuoka
S. 62 - 67	Tadao Ando
S. 68	Klaus Frahm / Contur GmbH
S. 70, 71	Studio Andreas Heller GmbH
S. 71	unten: Klaus Frahm / Contur GmbH
S. 72 - 75	Studio Andreas Heller GmbH
S. 76 - 83	Studio Matteo Thun
S. 84 - 91	Bitter+Bredt
S. 92 - 125	Mark Fisher

P. 12, 13	New Millennium Experience Co / QA Photos
P. 16, 17	Klaus Frahm / Contur GmbH
P. 20, 21	Bitter+Bredt
P. 24, 25	A. T. Schäfer
P. 28	New Millennium Experience Co / QA Photos
P. 31 - 33	Circus Krone
P. 35 - 37	Circus Roncalli
P. 38, 40	Annette Hauschild / Ostkreuz
P. 41	left: Annette Hauschild / Ostkreuz
	right: Jens Rötzsch / Ostkreuz
P. 42, 43	Plan: New Millennium Experience Co
P. 44, 45	Plan: New Millennium Experience Co
	top / right: New Millennium Experience Co / QA Photos
P. 46 - 49	New Millennium Experience Co / QA Photos
P. 50	Shinkenchiku-Sha / Mitsuo Matsuoka
P. 55, 57, 58	Studio Mario Botta
P. 56, 59	Alo Zanetta
P. 60	Shinkenchiku-Sha / Mitsuo Matsuoka
P. 62 - 67	Tadao Ando
P. 68	Klaus Frahm / Contur GmbH
P. 70, 71	Studio Andreas HellerGmbH
P. 71	below: Klaus Frahm / Contur GmbH
P. 72 - 75	Studio Andreas Heller GmbH
P. 76 - 83	Studio Matteo Thun
P. 84 - 91	Bitter+Bredt
P. 92 - 125	Mark Fisher

S. 126, 131 - 133	Mercedes-Benz / Wolfgang Wilhelm
S. 134	DaimlerChrysler / Andreas Keller
S. 136, 137	Plan: Kauffmann Theilig & Partner
S. 138 - 143	DaimlerChrysler / Andreas Keller
S. 144, 145	avstudios: Victor Brigola
S. 146	avstudios: Frank Erber
S. 147	links: DaimlerChrysler / Andreas Keller
	rechts: avstudios: Frank Erber
S. 148, 149	DaimlerChrysler / Vaclav Reischl
S. 150, 151	von links nach rechts:
	Berlin: Dirk Straub
	Stuttgart: DaimlerChrysler / Andreas Keller
	Hamburg / Neapel / Madrid: Andrea Wirges
S. 152	A. T. Schaefer
S. 156 - 159	Hans Dieter Schaal
S. 160 - 165	Bettina Müller
S. 166 - 171	Anita Pinggera
S. 172, 174	A. T. Schaefer
S. 175	Plan: Hans Dieter Schaal
S. 176 - 179	A. T. Schaefer
S. 180 - 183	Bregenzer Festspiele / Karl Forster
S. 184, 185	Bregenzer Festspiele / Foto Winsauer
S. 186	Bregenzer Festspiele / Karl Forster
S. 187	Bregenzer Festspiele / Foto Winsauer
S. 188 - 192	Bregenzer Festspiele / Karl Forster
S. 193	Bregenzer Festspiele / MOMA
S. 194, 195	Bregenzer Festspiele / Karl Forster

P. 126, 131 - 133	Mercedes-Benz / Wolfgang Wilhelm
P. 134	DaimlerChrysler / Andreas Keller
P. 136, 137	Plan: Kauffmann Theilig & Partner
P. 138 - 143	DaimlerChrysler / Andreas Keller
P. 144, 145	avstudios: Victor Brigola
P. 146	avstudios: Frank Erber
P. 147	left: DaimlerChrysler / Andreas Keller
	right: avstudios: Frank Erber
P. 148, 149	DaimlerChrysler / Vaclav Reischl
P. 150, 151	from left to right:
	Berlin: Dirk Straub
	Stuttgart: DaimlerChrysler / Andreas Keller
	Hamburg / Naples / Madrid: Andrea Wirges
P. 152	A. T. Schaefer
P. 156 - 159	Hans Dieter Schaal
P. 160 - 165	Bettina Müller
P. 166 - 171	Anita Pinggera
P. 172, 174	A. T. Schaefer
P. 175	Plan: Hans Dieter Schaal
P. 176 - 179	A. T. Schaefer
P. 180 - 183	Bregenzer Festspiele / Karl Forster
P. 184, 185	Bregenzer Festspiele / Foto Winsauer
P. 186	Bregenzer Festspiele / Karl Forster
P. 187	Bregenzer Festspiele / Foto Winsauer
P. 188 - 192	Bregenzer Festspiele / Karl Forster
P. 193	Bregenzer Festspiele / MOMA
P. 194, 195	Bregenzer Festspiele / Karl Forster

Impressum

Imprint

Konzept und Text	Dirk Meyhöfer
Recherche	Katja Borch
	Vineeta Manglani
Redaktion	Eva Wittwer
	Petra Kiedaisch
Gestaltung	**av**communication GmbH
	Claudia Stumpfe
Umschlagfoto	**av**communication GmbH
	Frank Erber: Millennium Dome, London
Übersetzung	Sean McLaughlin
Lithographie	**av**communication GmbH
	Corinna Rieber
Produktion	**av**communication GmbH
	Gunther Heeb
Druck	B+K Offsetdruck GmbH
Papier	Dullcoat, 150g/m²

Concept and Text	Dirk Meyhöfer
Research	Katja Borch
	Vineeta Manglani
Editors	Eva Wittwer
	Petra Kiedaisch
Design	**av**communication GmbH
	Claudia Stumpfe
Cover photograph	**av**communication GmbH
	Frank Erber: Millennium Dome, London
Translation	Sean McLaughlin
Lithography	**av**communication GmbH
	Corinna Rieber
Production	**av**communication GmbH
	Gunther Heeb
Printed by	B+K Offsetdruck GmbH
Paper	Dullcoat, 150g/m²

Die Deutsche Bibliothek - CIP-Einheitsaufnahme:
Mobile Bühnen = Mobile Stages / Dirk Meyhöfer.
[Red. Eva Wittwer ... Übers. Sean McLaughlin]. -
Stuttgart: av-Ed., 1999

ISBN 3-929638-24-X

Danksagung

Note of thanks

Mit freundlicher Unterstützung von:
Ambrosius Messebau GmbH, Frankfurt a. M.
DaimlerChrysler AG, Stuttgart

With the friendly support of:
Ambrosius Messebau GmbH, Frankfurt a. M.
DaimlerChrysler AG, Stuttgart

Wir senden Ihnen gerne unser Verlagsprogramm:

avedition GmbH
Reinsburgstraße 95 - 97
70197 Stuttgart
e-mail: kontakt@avedition.de

Unser Programm im Internet:
www.avedition.de

We would be pleased to send you our catalogue:

avedition GmbH
Reinsburgstraße 95 - 97
70197 Stuttgart
e-mail: kontakt@avedition.de

Our catalogue can also be viewed on the Internet:
www.avedition.de